DEAD MAN WALKING

by the same author

BOB ROBERTS
(Published in *Projections 2*)

DEAD MAN WALKING

Tim Robbins

Based on the book *Dead Man Walking*
by Sister Helen Prejean, CSJ

faber and faber
LONDON · BOSTON

First published in 1996
by Faber and Faber Limited
3 Queen Square London WC1N 3AU

Photoset by Parker Typesetting Service, Leicester
Printed in England by Clays Ltd, St Ives plc

A CIP record for this book
is available from the British Library
ISBN 0-571-17971-1

2 4 6 8 10 9 7 5 3 1

CONTENTS

Tim Robbins with Director of Photography Roger Deakins

Sister Helen Prejean with Tim Robbins

Dead Man Walking opened in the UK on 29 March 1996.

The cast and crew includes:

SISTER HELEN PREJEAN	Susan Sarandon
MATTHEW PONCELET	Sean Penn
HILTON BARBER	Robert Prosky
EARL DELACROIX	Raymond J. Barry
CLYDE PERCY	R. Lee Ermey
MARY BETH PERCY	Celia Weston
HELEN'S MOTHER	Lois Smith
CHAPLAIN FARLEY	Scott Wilson
LUCILLE PONCELET	Roberta Maxwell
SISTER COLLEEN	Margo Martindale
CAPTAIN BELIVEAU	Barton Heyman
SGT NEAL TRAPP	Steve Boles
WARDEN HARTMAN	Nesbitt Blaisdell
LUIS MONTOYA	Ray Aranha
GUY GILARDI	Larry Pine
BISHOP NORWICH	Gil Robbins
GOVERNOR BENEDICT	Kevin Cooney
STATE TROOPER	Clancy Brown
NURSE	Adele Robbins
CARL VITELLO	Michael Cullen
WALTER DELACROIX	Peter Sarsgaard
HOPE PERCY	Missy Yager
EMILY PERCY	Jenny Krochmal

Director of Photography	Roger Deakins
Production Design	Richard Hoover
Costume Design	Renee Ehrlich Kalfus
Edited by	Lisa Zeno Churgin
Music by	David Robbins
Screenplay by	Tim Robbins

Consultant	Sister Helen Prejean, CSJ
Executive Producers	Tim Bevan Eric Fellner
Produced by	Jon Kilik Tim Robbins Rudd Simmons
Directed by	Tim Robbins

A Working Title/Havoc Production released by Polygram Filmed Entertainment

For
Lee Robbins
and
Thelma Bledsoe

INT. PREJEAN CAR. DAY. SISTER HELEN PREJEAN DRIVES

Sister Helen belies our standard image of nuns in movies. She is presently, in fact, anonymous, forgoing the traditional habit for a practical, simple dress. In fact, the only thing suggesting religion is the simple silver crucifix she wears around her neck. The shadows of trees fall across her face as she drives.

FLASHBACK – INT. CHURCH. DAY

A woman looks down; the camera pulls back, panning to a bride, a young Helen, surrounded by her maid of honor and her mother. They all wave as children run in front of them. The maid of honor helps put on young Helen's white glove.

'The Face of Love' plays on the soundtrack.

EXT. HOPE HOUSE. DAY

Boys running; girls twirling batons and skipping ropes.

Overlapping chatter of school kids.

Helen walks at a brisk pace carrying two grocery bags. She has a strong, confident walk; this is a woman with work to do. The neighborhood has seen better days, but there is a warmth here, a sense of community.

KENITRA

Hi, Sister Prejean.

HELEN

Hi, Kenitra. How ya doin'?

Helen walks up the front steps of the Hope House. The sign hanging above the door reads:

HOPE HOUSE

Helen exits into the building.

INT. HOPE HOUSE. DAY

A woman, Idella, sits at her desk in a classroom of students. Helen enters and puts her things down. Idella looks at her.

IDELLA
(*chuckles*)
Well, if it ain't the late Sister Helen.

HELEN
I've got a note from my mama, Idella.

Helen walks to Idella and hands her a composition book.

Do you need a new composition book?

IDELLA
Sure, thanks.

Helen looks at Melvin.

HELEN
How 'bout you, Melvin?

Helen walks to Sister Colleen.

COLLEEN
The Resident Council wants us to come to their meeting tomorrow. Can you be there at seven?

A man, Luis Montoya, enters through the doorway and walks toward Helen.

HELEN
(*gasps*)
Yes. New poetry books.

Helen takes a booklet from the sister.

COLLEEN
Your, your poem got all smudged.

HELEN
Smudged?

COLLEEN

Hmm.

Montoya walks up behind Helen, who looks through the new poetry book.

MONTOYA

Sister Helen, I got another letter from that guy I was telling you about.

HELEN

Which guy is that, Luis?

MONTOYA

Angola inmate, Death Row.

Helen glances over her shoulder at Montoya.

HELEN

Oh, yeah, yeah. Uh-huh.

MONTOYA

I was wondering if you could write to him. Sounds like he could use some friendly words.

HELEN

Sure, sure. I – I – I'll come up after the class.

Montoya exits as Helen and Colleen look down at the poetry book.

MONTOYA
(*overlapping*)

Okay.

HELEN

It got smudged.

COLLEEN

You can still read it.

INT. CAR. DAY

Helen drives. The shadows of trees fall against her face.

INT. HOPE HOUSE. DAY

Helen teaches a high school equivalency class. She is alongside a student, Idella, who is reading, using a ruler to follow along on the page. Helen bends over Idella, listening to her read.

IDELLA
(*reading*)

There's a woman standing there in the dark. And she's got big arms to hold you, but you won't feel those arms that hug . . .

FLASHBACK – INT. CHURCH. DAY

A bride (torso only), holding a lit candle, walks across screen, revealing a little girl and another bride, Helen, followed by another little girl and yet another bride. All walk in line, holding lit candles.

IDELLA
(*voice-over*)

. . . till you can see her face. So you stand there waiting for the . . .

Six brides face the altar and kneel in front of the bishop performing the ceremony.

. . . light at the end of the road.

HELEN
(*voice-over; gasps*)

Idella, that is . . .

The camera tilts down from the arched church ceiling to one of the brides, young Helen.

. . . so fine.

IDELLA
(*voice-over*)

Thank you.

INT. PREJEAN APARTMENT. NIGHT

Through the window we see kids hanging out in the alley outside. Helen sits at her desk looking down at a letter. Montoya looks over her shoulder.

MATT
(*voice-over*)
My lawyer seems to have disappeared. So I could use some help on the legal end, but if you can't do that, I'd take a kind word or a visit. Gets real quiet here sometimes.

MONTOYA
'Course, none of these guys on the Row can afford their own attorneys for appeals.

INT. PREJEAN APARTMENT. KITCHEN. NIGHT

Helen sits at the table writing a letter.

MONTOYA
(*off*)
You can imagine the frantic telephone calls we get from Death Row inmates . . .

Helen (hands only) inserts a letter and two snapshots (one, the sunset over the bay, the other of her and a dog) into an envelope and turns the envelope over to reveal the address.

. . . begging us to find them attorneys.

HELEN
(*off*)
Who'll work for nothing.

MONTOYA
(*off*)
That's right. These petitions take hours and hours to prepare. Attorneys aren't exactly lining up outside the door for the job.

The letterhead reads:

MATTHEW PONCELET
LA STATE PRISON

INT. CAR. DAY

Helen drives. The shadows of trees fall against her face.

FLASHBACK – INT. CHURCH. DAY

Young Helen is now dressed in traditional nun attire. She and two other nuns kneel down and pray.

INT. PREJEAN APARTMENT. BEDROOM. DAY

Helen holds Matt's letter and picture.

MATT
(*voice-over*)
'Dear Sister Helen, thank you for writing to me, I'm writing . . .'

On Helen sitting on the bed reading Matt's letter.

'. . . from my home, my six-by-eight-foot cell.'

EXT. LOUISIANA HIGHWAY. DAY

Helen's car travels up the road.

MATT
(*voice-over*)
'I'm in here twenty-three hours a day.'

FLASHBACK – EXT. CHURCH. DAY

Young Sister Helen stands on the front steps between her sister and her mother. She hugs her mother and then her sister. The three wave to the camera. Other parishioners are in the background.

MATT
(*voice-over*)
'We don't work on Death Row. We're special here. They keep us away from the general population of the prison. We're the elite, 'cause we gonna fry. It's hard . . .'

INT. CAR. DAY

Helen drives.

MATT

(*voice–over*)

'. . . not to get soft in this cell. I press my foot locker, lift it . . .'

Through the windshield Helen passes a billboard that reads:

GET TOUGH!
TEAM UP WITH
GOVERNOR BEN BENEDICT
TO STAMP OUT CRIME

'. . . to try to get my muscles in shape. But it's hard not to get fat.'

Helen drives.

'Rice, potatoes . . .'

EXT. LOUISIANA HIGHWAY. DAY

Helen's car travels up a road and disappears around a curve.

MATT

(*voice-over*)

'. . . pancakes, beans. Sometimes I feel like a sow on a farm that's being fattened up for a Christmas slaughter.'

FLASHBACK – EXT. CHURCH. DAY.

Young Sister Helen stands between her mother and her sister as it starts to rain. Her sister, mother and other parishioners hurry up the steps to get under the roof. Young Sister Helen, undaunted by the rain, smiles and waves to the camera, then walks up the steps towards the others.

MATT

(*voice-over*)

'I had a dream once that I was about to be fried in the chair and then this guy come into my cell with a chef's hat on and started to roll me around in breadcrumbs . . .'

EXT. ANGOLA PRISON GATE. DAY

Helen's car enters and travels towards the prison guard gate. The roof reads:

LOUISIANA STATE
PENITENTIARY

MATT

(*voice-over*)

'. . . crumbs, lickin' his chops and all. Maybe you think I'm a weirdo to have dreams like that, but your mind does . . .'

INT. VISITOR ENTRANCE. DAY

Helen (hand only) drops her keys into a plastic box; a Prison Guard (torso only) takes her purse.

MATT

(*voice-over*)

'. . . funny things when you're locked up and surrounded by people that wanna kill you.'

Helen looks at the Guard, who checks her purse.

PRISON GUARD

Step in.

Helen walks through the metal detector, which beeps as she walks through.

MATT

(*voice-over*)

'Anyway, thanks for writing. I don't get many letters, visitors either. No one in my family seems able to make the trip out here. I understand. It's a long drive from Slidell.'

A female guard enters and pats Helen down, as another guard tips in and scans a metal detector over the crucifix that hangs around Helen's neck.

INT. CHAPLAIN'S OFFICE. DAY

Chaplain Farley enters and walks towards Helen, who is sitting facing his desk.

FARLEY

Good morning.

HELEN

Good morning, Father.

Helen stands and looks at Farley as they shake hands.

FARLEY

Sister . . .

HELEN

Helen Prejean. Nice to meet you.

FARLEY

Have a seat.

HELEN

Thank you.

Helen sits down. Farley sits at his desk and looks at Helen.

FARLEY

Have you been in a prison before?

HELEN

No . . .

Helen looks at Farley.

. . . Father. Sister Clement and I sang at the Juvenile Detention Center in New Orleans. We sang 'Kumbaya' and the boys really liked it. They started making up their own verses, singing, 'Someone's escapin', my Lord. Kum – ' (*Laughs.*) The guards made us sing a different song.

Farley touches a small plant on his desk as he speaks.

FARLEY
(*chuckles*)

Where is your habit?

HELEN

Our sisters haven't worn the habit for twenty years, Father.

FARLEY

You are aware of the Papal request regarding nuns' garments, aren't you?

HELEN

I believe the Pope said 'distinctive clothing', not habits.

Farley looks at Helen and then down at the letter he holds.

FARLEY

Well, I'm sure you will interpret it in your own way. Whatever's convenient. Matthew Poncelet. I remember him from the news. Him and another fellah. Shot two children in the back of the head on a lovers' lane. Raped the girl, stabbed her several times. Do you know what you're gettin' into?

Helen swallows hard.

So what is it, Sister? Morbid fascination? Bleeding heart sympathy?

HELEN

He wrote me and asked me to come.

FARLEY

There is no romance here, Sister. No Jimmy Cagney, 'I've been wrongly accused. If I only had someone who believed in me' nonsense. They are all con men. And they will take advantage of you every way they can. You must be very, very careful. Do you understand?

HELEN

Yes, Father.

EXT. ANGOLA PRISON. DAY

Through a chain-link fence, the camera dollies past the guard tower.

FARLEY

(*voice-over*)

These men don't see many females. For you to wear the habit . . .

Through a chain-link gate, a guard looks at Helen, who looks up at the guard tower. She walks towards the gate as the guard (arm only) tips in and opens the gate. Helen walks through, followed by the guard, who closes the gate behind.

. . . might help instill respect. For you to flout authority will only encourage them to do the same.

FLASHBACK – EXT. LOUISIANA WOODS. NIGHT

A person can be seen sitting in a parked car in the middle of the woods.

EXT. ANGOLA PRISON. DAY

Helen and the guard (their legs only) walk.

FLASHBACK – EXT. LOUISIANA WOODS. NIGHT

A person can be seen sitting in the parked car.

EXT. ANGOLA PRISON. DAY

Helen and the guard walk down the sidewalk.

FLASHBACK – EXT. LOUISIANA WOODS. NIGHT

The barrel of a shotgun moves into frame, pointing down.

EXT. ANGOLA PRISON. DAY

Helen walks down the sidewalk. Through chain-linked fences she sees two inmates playing ball.

FLASHBACK – EXT. LOUISIANA WOODS. NIGHT

Lightning flashes, illuminating the trees.

INT. DEATH ROW BUILDING. DAY

Helen and the guard walk through Death Row.

PRISON GUARD
(*shouts*)

Woman on the tier!

Another guard enters and opens the gate. Helen and the escorting guard walk through the gate, which is closed behind them.

FLASHBACK – EXT. LOUISIANA WOODS. NIGHT

A muddy body (leg only) lies motionless on the ground.

The low chatter of the inmates continues under following scenes.

A second muddy body (legs only) lies motionless on the ground.

INT. DEATH ROW. DAY

Helen walks through a door that the guard holds open for her. It reads:

VISITING ROOM

FLASHBACK – EXT. LOUISIANA WOODS. NIGHT

A body (torso and hand only) lies motionless, face down on the ground.

INT. DEATH ROW. DAY

A guard (torso only) unlocks a barred door, and Helen walks through. She walks toward a guard behind the mesh screen.

VISITING ROOM GUARD

You can wait over there. We'll bring your man out for ya.

Helen nods and sits down.

Off; overlapping low shouts and chatter of inmates and visitors.

A prisoner in chains enters escorted by a guard. The camera moves in on Helen, who looks visibly shaken.

FLASHBACK – EXT. LOUISIANA WOODS. NIGHT

A person (torso and hand only) lifts a bloody dagger over his head and thrusts it down.

INT. DEATH ROW. DAY

Through mesh screen we see an inmate, Matthew Poncelet, enter and look at Helen, who smiles at him. He sits down.

HELEN

Well, Matthew, I made it.

MATT

Thanks for coming, ma'am. Humph. Never thought I'd be visiting with no nun.

Matt lights a cigarette. His hands are chained.

So you're a nun.

HELEN

Yep.

Matt looks away and snickers.

And I just want you to know, I'm here to listen, and whatever you want to talk about, that's fine.

MATT

You're very sincere.

HELEN

What do you mean?

MATT

You never done this before?

HELEN

No.

MATT

Never been this close to a murderer before?

HELEN

Not that I know of.

MATT

(*off*)

Hmm. You live in St Thomas. Lots of niggers down there. They knock each other off like beer cans off a fence. You know when I got your letter, I seen Helen on it. I thought it was my first ex-old lady. Almost ripped it up.

(*on Matt*)

She turned me in, called the cops. Orphaned our kid, the stupid bitch.

HELEN

You've got a kid?

MATT

Yeah, a con with a kid.

HELEN

Girl or boy?

MATT

Girl.

HELEN

What's her name?

MATT

You ask a lot of questions.

HELEN

I don't know you.

MATT

Yeah, well never mind.

Matt bends down to take a drag of his cigarette.

Hmm. In your letter you say you work with poor people. Your daddy was a lawyer? Yeah? You come from money, don't you?

HELEN

Some.

MATT

Hmm. And you live in St Thomas Projects? I don't get that. I don't know who's crazier, you or me?

HELEN

I live where I work.

MATT

Yeah, in a slum.

HELEN

What about you?

MATT

I live here.

HELEN

You were brought up poor?

MATT

Ain't nobody with money on Death Row.

HELEN

Then you and I have something in common.

MATT

What's that?

HELEN

We both live with the poor.

MATT

Hmm. Humph. Ain't you gonna ask me what I done?

HELEN

The chaplain filled me in.

MATT

Oh, Farley? He's a very religious man.

Helen smiles.

I didn't kill nobody. Carl went crazy on me.

HELEN

Carl?

MATT

Vitello. He oughta be sittin' here. Went nuts on me. I was scared, did what he said, held that boy back. But he killed 'em.

HELEN

You watched him kill these kids?

MATT

(*off*)

I'll tell you the truth, ma'am.

(*on Matt*)

Me and Carl were loaded on downs and acid and booze when this happened.

Helen listens.

I hadn't slept in two nights. I was outta my head. But I didn't kill 'em. I didn't kill nobody. I swear to God I didn't.

Through the sun-drenched meshed screen, Helen squints to see Matt.

FLASHBACK – EXT. LOUISIANA WOODS. NIGHT

A naked female body (arm and thigh only) lies motionless on the ground.

INT. DEATH ROW. DAY

Through the sun-drenched mesh screen we see Matt's face.

FLASHBACK – EXT. LOUISIANA WOODS. NIGHT

A naked female body (leg only) lies motionless on the ground.

MATT
(*voice-over*)

Allie.

INT. DEATH ROW. DAY

Through the sun-drenched mesh screen, we see Matt's face.

FLASHBACK – EXT. LOUISIANA WOODS. NIGHT

A naked female body (legs only) lies motionless on the ground.

INT. DEATH ROW. DAY

Through mesh screen, Matt (hands only) holds a picture of a little girl.

HELEN

Allie?

MATT

Her name.

Helen leans forward for a better look.

HELEN

Oh . . . she's cute.

MATT

She's eleven or twelve, I don't know. She was born when I was in prison the first time. I seen her once.

HELEN

When was that?

MATT

When she was three.

HELEN

Do you write to her?

MATT

I don't know where she is. She's in Texas somewhere. Foster parents.

VISITING ROOM GUARD

(off)

You wanna . . .

Helen glances over her shoulder at the guard.

. . . finish up now, Sister.

Helen nods and looks back at Matt. The guard exits.

Through mesh screen, Matt leans forward.

MATT

Look.

Helen listens.

MATT

They're about to go on a killing spree here. They gonna zap this guy Tobias tonight. The guards are taking bets on who's next. I'm at even odds, not good. So the way I see it, I got two chances: the pardon board and a federal appeals court. Now, I wrote the motion on the appeal, but I need somebody to file it. Can you help me with that?

HELEN

You know how to write a motion?

Helen sits back.

MATT

Well, when your back's against the wall you learn the law real fast. Call it special motivation. I've been on Death Row six years. I've read and studied every law book I can get my hands on. I got all this stuff here about my case, transcripts of the trial . . .

Helen's POV. Through the mesh screen. The transcripts sit on the counter in front of Matt (hands only).

. . . legal papers. Maybe they'd help you get a hold of the things about me and my case a little faster. You drop a dime and wrestle me up a lawyer who can file a motion for appeal.

Through the mesh screen Matt looks at Helen.

Through the mesh screen Helen looks at Matt.

Through the mesh screen Matt looks at Helen.

You ain't comin' back, are ya?

HELEN

No, I just . . . Uh, are these your only copies?

MATT

I got my own copy, but they're hard to come by, so if you ain't gonna help me, I don't wanna waste 'em on you.

HELEN

I'll do my best. And I appreciate your trust.

Through mesh screen. A guard (torso only) enters and stands behind Matt, who looks at Helen.

MATT

I'll tell ya somethin', Sister, I don't trust nobody in here.

At the visitor guard station Helen is signing a list. A guard (hands only) hands her a folder and she walks out.

(*voice-over*)

But you come down here and don't kiss my ass or preach that hellfire and brimstone crap. I respect that. You got guts.

INT. CAR. DAY

Helen drives.

MATT

(*voice-over*)

Hell, you live in a neighborhood with every nigger carryin' a gun.

Helen drives past trees.

OPOSSUM KID I

(*voice-over*)

Come on, Helen, hit it!

FLASHBACK – EXT. PREJEAN MOTHER'S HOME (1955). DAY

The camera pans off the trees to a young girl, nine-year-old Helen, who looks down, beating an opossum with a stick, grunting with the effort.

OPOSSUM KIDS

Yay! Yay!

Overlapping cheers and shouts continue under the following scenes.

Cut to camera dollying from behind the trees to reveal nine-year-old Helen and two other children running, wielding sticks.

INT. CAR. DAY

Helen passes by the trees at the side of the road.

FLACKBACK – EXT. PREJEAN MOTHER'S HOME (1955). DAY

Nine-year-old Helen and two other children run. Waving sticks in the air.

Cut to an opossum lying motionless on the ground, 'playing possum'. Five children holding sticks tip in around it.

Cut to nine-year-old Helen and two other children running.

INT. CAR. DAY

Helen drives. The sun is shining through the trees alongside the road.

FLASHBACK – EXT. PREJEAN MOTHER'S HOME (1955). DAY

A boy lifts up a stick and smashes it down on the opossum.

Cut to another boy beating the opossum.

Cut to nine-year-old Helen staring down at the opossum.

OPOSSUM KID 2

Playin' possum, huh? You think you can . . .

Cut to nine-year-old Helen and the other children. They surround the opossum and beat it with their sticks.

. . . trick us, you dumb animal? Think you can fool us?

INT. CAR. DAY

In the rearview mirror a police car appears, sirens on.

Helen drives towards the side of the road.

In the rearview mirror, the police car comes to a stop.

EXT. LOUISIANA HIGHWAY/INT. HELEN'S CAR. DAY

A state trooper looks down at Helen, who sits in her car and hands him her license.

HELEN

How fast was I going?

STATE TROOPER

Seventy-five miles an hour, ma'am.

HELEN

Wow.

STATE TROOPER

You a nun?

HELEN

Yessir.

STATE TROOPER

Never gave a ticket to no nun before. Gave a ticket to a guy from the IRS one time. Got audited the next year.

The trooper looks down at Helen and hands back her license.

STATE TROOPER

Tell ya what, Sister, I'm gonna let this one slide. But you keep your speed down, ya hear?

HELEN

Yes, sir.

INT. PRISON COALITION. DAY

Helen (torso only) sits at her desk reading a transcript.

Cut to Helen (hand only) holding the minutes from Matt's trial, camera tilting down to newspaper clippings picturing Matt. The headlines read:

JURY RECOMMENDS DEATH PENALTY IN PONCELET TRIAL
KILLER APPEALS
TRIAL SET FOR SLAY SUSPECT

REPORTER 1
(voice-over)

On Friday night, Walter Delacroix, age seventeen, and Hope Percy, eighteen, had been just two happy people celebrating one of life's turning points.

Cut to static on a TV screen. Then a newspaper clipping pictures a teenage girl and a teenage boy, their names, Hope Percy and Walter Delacroix, are below their pictures.

REPORTER 2
(voice-over)

The couple were shot twice at close range . . .

Then, on the TV, a reporter speaks into a microphone.

. . . in the back of the head with a twenty-two caliber rifle.

The TV picture turns to static, then Matt walks in, surrounded by guards.

REPORTER 3
(voice-over, overlapping)

In addition to murder charges, Poncelet and Vitello face six counts of aggravated kidnapping and one charge of aggravated rape.

The TV screen turns to static, then a female reporter speaks into a microphone.

FEMALE REPORTER
(voice-over, overlapping)
. . . would handcuff the man and molest the woman . . .

REPORTER 3
(on screen)
. . . in the last four weeks before the murder the two accused men allegedly had cut . . .

On the TV screen, Matt sits in court miming cutting someone's throat.

(voice-over)
. . . a wide path of terror across the area, attacking several teenage couples . . .

REPORTER 4
(voice-over, overlapping)
. . . come forward.

REPORTER 3
(voice-over)
. . . in local lovers' lanes.

The TV screen turns to static, then another reporter speaks into his microphone.

REPORTER 4
A police spokesman said today though, in the wake of the murders . . .

The TV screen turns to static.

Then a newspaper clipping picturing Matt's lawyer, and then Matt's image appears on the TV screen.

REPORTER 3
(voice-over, overlapping)
Matthew Poncelet addressed the judge as 'Cap' and smirked when the jury found him guilty of murder today.

Helen looks at Montoya.

HELEN

Poncelet claims Vitello killed both of them.

Montoya sits at his desk, looking at Helen. He chuckles.

Y'all think he's lying.

MONTOYA

Vitello accuses Poncelet. Both say the other did the actual killing. Somebody's lying to somebody. Heh. They were both there. We know that much.

HELEN

Well, then how is it possible one guy gets life, the other death?

MONTOYA

Well, the state probably had a stronger case against Poncelet. Vitello had a better lawyer. Created a reasonable doubt in the jury's mind.

HELEN

And Vitello gets life, Poncelet death.

MONTOYA

Yeah.

HELEN

Bad luck.

MONTOYA

He needs help, Sister. There's this lawyer, Hilton Barber, he's aware of the case, he told me no. Maybe you can change his mind?

HELEN

With the aim of getting him a new trial and getting him out? I'm not so sure I want to run into this guy on the street.

MONTOYA

There's no way he's gettin' off. He was there, he was an accomplice. That's life. Life sentences in a Louisiana prison is for real. We're just trying to stop the state from killing him.

Helen hangs her head.

Montoya looks at Helen.

You want out? It's cool with me. You don't have to go back there.

INT. PREJEAN APARTMENT. NIGHT

On the TV, Governor Benedict speaks from behind a podium.

BENEDICT
(*on screen*)

Get tough on sentencing. Get tough on lenient parole boards. Get tough on judges who pass light sentences.

Sister Colleen and Helen sit on the sofa watching the TV.

Benedict's TV speech continues low and indistinct under the conversation.

The phone rings. Helen answers it.

HELEN
(*into phone*)

Hello.

MATT
(*over phone*)

Sister Helen?

HELEN

Who's this?

MATT

Matt Poncelet.

Helen gestures to Sister Colleen to turn off the TV. Colleen crosses to TV.

I didn't know who to call. I know I'm on Death Row, but there's guys been here years and years. I didn't know this was coming. They set a date.

HELEN

What?

MATT

They're gonna kill me. It's gonna go down on the thirteenth. I gotta do somethin'. I didn't know you needed a lawyer to get a pardon board hearing. Hell, I'd do it myself if they'd let me, but they say, 'No lawyer, no hearing'.

HELEN
(*overlapping*)

Okay. Okay. Okay, Matthew. Uh, I think I know of a lawyer that may be able to help you. And I'll do my best, all right?

MATT

Sister, come through for me. You're all I got. They got me on a greased rail to the death house here. I ain't heard from you. You ain't fading out on me, are you, Sister?

HELEN

I'll get you the lawyer, just try not to worry.

Sister Colleen looks at Helen, camera tilting down to the TV on which Clyde Percy now speaks.

(*off*)

I'll call you soon.

MATT
(*overlapping*)

Bye.

HELEN
(*off*)

Bye.

CLYDE
(*on screen, overlapping*)

. . . six years. As far as I'm concerned, it's about time the State got with the program. Call me sentimental, but I'd rather see 'em fry.

The picture switches to an anchorman.

ANCHORMAN
(*on screen*)

Barring any last minute appeals or stays, Poncelet will die under . . .

On the TV there is a photo of Matt.

. . . the state's new execution procedure, the lethal injection machine.

The picture switches to a shot of the lethal injection machine.

Helen makes a phone call.

HELEN

Ah, Luis, this is Helen. Can you tell me the name of that lawyer you wanted me talk to?

INT. HELEN'S CAR. DAY

Hilton Barber sits in the passenger seat as Helen drives.

HILTON

How long you been doing this, Sister?

HELEN

Doing this?

HILTON

Counseling Death Row inmates.

HELEN

Oh, I'm not counseling him. I . . . I hardly know him. I just met him once.

HILTON

What's your impression?

HELEN

I don't know if I like him. He needs help, and I figured the best thing I could do is bring him you.

HILTON

Well, I'll do my best.

Helen looks at Hilton.

EXT. LOUISIANA HIGHWAY. DAY

Through the trees, Helen's car enters and travels along the road. Then it disappears behind the brush.

HILTON

(*voice-over*)

Courts don't want to hear appeals on death penalty cases. Hell . . .

INT. HELEN'S CAR. DAY

Helen drives.

HILTON

. . . you can even have new evidence of innocence and the court won't hear the case. We're the pariahs.

Through the windshield. The car travels past a sign that reads:

HAVE MANY
RABBIT
⟶

We're . . . 'Have Many Rabbit'.

HELEN

Think that's a For Sale sign or a cry for help?

HILTON

(*chuckles*)

. . . Or is he bragging?

HELEN

(*laughs*)

Imagine that poor guy. Bought two rabbits a year ago and now he's overrun.

HILTON

(*laughs*)

Comin' like popcorn.

INT. DEATH ROW. DAY

Through a mesh screen, Matt looks at Hilton.

MATT

The day before Governor Benedict is gonna run for re-election they set a date for my execution. Show how tough he is on crime.

HILTON

All right, I agree with you. Politics did play a big part in this decision, but the pardon board, that's not a place to bring this up.

MATT

Why not?

Hilton and Helen look at Matt.

HILTON

Because it's full of political appoin –

Matt looks away, annoyed.

– tees. The Governor's appointees. And the last thing they want to hear is some convicted killer telling them they is bunk. What we have to do is present you as a person, a human being, and convince them to spare your life.

MATT

What we have to do is prove I'm innocent.

HILTON

We're gettin' to that. We're filing appeals with the Federal Court, uh, the Supreme Court, but this is a pardon board. Now, it don't mean a thing to them . . . whether you pulled the trigger or not, they're gonna be thinking of the crime. And of you as a monster.

Matt shakes his head.

Now, it's easy to kill a monster, but it's hard to kill a human being. That's why we need people that know you, like your mama . . .

Matt looks away.

. . . to speak on your behalf. Now, your mama should be at this hearing.

MATT

I don't want her there. She's just gonna bust out cryin' till she can't say nothing, she gonna be so tore up.

HILTON

Be that as it may, your mama should still be there.

MATT

(*overlapping*)

No, no. She's gonna have to hear the Delacroixs, the Percys, the DA. No.

HILTON

(*overlapping*)

Look, if she's not at the hearing, we might as well . . .

HELEN

(*interrupting*)

Excuse me for buttin' in. You're right, it's gonna be upsetting for her, but she's your mama, Matthew, your mama. She should have the opportunity to speak for her child if she wants to.

MATT

She's just gonna blubber her head off.

HELEN

Yeah, well, she has the right to do that. What if you die and she hasn't had a chance to speak for ya? Don't you think it's always gonna eat at her wonderin' if she could have saved you?

MATT

(*sighs*)

I'll think about it, but I want you all to know I got my pride. I ain't gonna kiss ass in front of these people. I ain't gonna kiss nobody's ass.

INT. PREJEAN'S APARTMENT. DAY

Colleen sits laughing with four children around a coffee table cluttered with art supplies and paper. Helen sits in a chair reading newspaper clippings.

COLLEEN

(*laughs*)

What are you making, Kenitra?

KENITRA

An Easter card for my mama.

COLLEEN

What's that?

KENITRA

(*off*)

That's an Easter bunny going down a chimney.

Helen (hand only) holds the newspaper article. The headline reads:

PARENTS' GRIEF NEVER ENDS

Gospel music plays.

INT. CHURCH. DAY

The camera tilts down from the arched ceiling of the church to reveal a gospel choir singing at the altar. A parishioner carrying a cross enters.

The congregation claps and sings as robed altar persons walk down the aisle.

A row of parishioners are clapping; the camera pans to the row behind them to reveal Sister Colleen and Helen, who clap along and sing.

CONGREGATION

(*singing*)

'This is the day that the Lord has made . . .'

Music continues indistinct under the following scenes.

The gospel choir faces the congregation. All sing and clap.

Two young boys clap.

A section of the gospel choir claps and sings.

'This is the day that the Lord has made . . .'

The choir director directs the gospel choir.

EXT. PONCELET HOUSE. DAY

Helen walks down the sidewalk towards a dilapidated house.

Gospel song continues low and indistinct under the following two scenes.

Helen looks at Matt's brother, Craig Poncelet, who leans against a car he has been working on.

HELEN

Happy Easter.

Craig looks at Helen.

Helen knocks at the front door. She looks down at Craig, who turns around and resumes working on his car.

LUCILLE
(*off*)

Yes?

Helen speaks through the door.

HELEN

Mrs Poncelet?

LUCILLE
(*off*)

No.

HELEN

Mrs Poncelet, please.

LUCILLE
(*off*)

Don't live here. Who is it?

HELEN

My name is Sister Helen Prejean. Uh, I know your son Matthew.

The door opens and Lucille Poncelet peeks out.

Happy Easter.

LUCILLE

You sure you're a Sister?

HELEN

Yes.

LUCILLE

You're not from the TV.

HELEN

No.

LUCILLE

You're sure?

Helen nods.

HELEN

Um-hm.

LUCILLE

How do you know Mattie?

HELEN

I met him on Death Row.

INT. PONCELET HOUSE. TV ROOM. DAY.

Matt's two other brothers, Troy and Sonny Poncelet, watch the TV.

LUCILLE
(*off*)

Well, you never know who's at your front door.

INT. PONCELET KITCHEN. DAY

Lucille sits at the kitchen table looking at Helen, who sits across from her.

LUCILLE

So, what do you want? Mattie send you for money, for cigarettes?

Helen looks at Lucille and shakes her head.

HELEN
(*chuckles*)

No.

LUCILLE

So what do you want?

HELEN

You know they, they set the date for Matthew's execution.

LUCILLE

Yeah. Prison called, said if it goes down, do I got Death Insurance? Hah! What a laugh. I ain't even got food money.

HELEN

His pardon board hearing is this Wednesday and his lawyer thinks it'd be a good idea if you were there.

LUCILLE

What does Mattie think?

HELEN

He's worried. He wants to protect you.

LUCILLE

Well, it's a little late for that. That show *Inside Crime* did a thing on Mattie and told how I tried to help him and everything. A regular Ma Barker or something. Now I'm famous. Yesterday I was in the store and I see these two ladies eyeing me, and when I get closer I hear one of them say, 'I just can't wait to hear that they have executed that monster Matthew Poncelet.'

HELEN

That's cruel.

LUCILLE

My boys are havin' a real hard time at school. Kids pickin' on 'em, beatin' 'em up, callin' 'em names.

INT. PONCELET HOUSE. TV ROOM. DAY

Troy and Sonny sit on the couch looking at the TV.

LUCILLE

(off)

Someone put a dead squirrel inside my little Troy's locker. Poor boy came home cryin'.

INT. PONCELET HOUSE. KITCHEN. DAY

Lucille looks at Helen.

LUCILLE

What'd he ever do to anyone?

Helen looks at Lucille.

Lucille looks at Helen.

I just keep tryin' to figure out what I done wrong.

EXT. PREJEAN HOUSE. NIGHT

A well-appointed middle-class Southern home.

HELEN

(*voice-over*)

These people have been plowed over by life.

INT. PREJEAN HOUSE. DINING ROOM. NIGHT

Helen sits at the dinner table with her family. She talks to her brother, Louis, who sits across from her.

HELEN

He started gettin' in trouble when he was fifteen.

LOUIS

Every kid gets into trouble when he's fifteen.

HELEN

His daddy was never around.

LOUIS

Helen, most of your kids in the projects are raised by single parents. They're not raping and killing people. Really, Helen, you're being suckered.

HELEN

There you go again, Louis.

LOUIS

I mean, what about the parents of these victims? Are, are you seeing them? Have you counseled them?

HELEN

You think they'd want to talk to me?

MOTHER

Aren't there people in your neighborhood that need your help? Honest people?

HELEN

Yes, Mama. I'm still working with them.

MOTHER

But why are you visiting with murderers? They're the end of the line people. For all the energy and resources that you're putting into them, you could be keeping other kids from going to prison and Death Row.

HELEN'S SISTER

Uh, Mama's friends, the Pierres, they read an article which mentioned your name as being associated with Poncelet.

HELEN

My name was in the paper?

MOTHER

It has nothing to do with that. I am simply curious. Helen, what has drawn you to this?

Helen looks at her mother.

HELEN

Mama, I don't know. I feel caught more than drawn. The man's in trouble and, for some reason, I'm the only one he trusts.

MOTHER

I know your heart's in the right place, Helen, but a full heart shouldn't follow an empty head.

LOUIS

Or an empty stomach.

Helen smiles at her mother.

HELEN

Oh!

Helen tosses her napkin at her brother. Louis catches the napkin. Helen's sister and other family members smile. Louis chuckles.

MOTHER

When you were a child you were always bringing home strays.

Helen sighs.

If we'd taken in all those dogs and cats we wouldn't have had any money to feed the children in this house. Your heart is large. Just take care that others don't take advantage of it. I'd hate to see that.

Helen looks at her mother.

HELEN

All right, Mama.

INT. DEATH ROW. DAY

Through mesh screen, Matt looks at Helen.

MATT

My daddy took me to a bar when I was twelve and told me to pick my whiskey, so, there was all these bottles behind the bar, and I pointed up there and I said, 'I'll take that one there with the pretty turkey on it.' The guys in the bar laughed their butts off. We got drunk as a couple of coots that night. My daddy was a good man. Sharecropper, hard worker. That's the one thing I got from him: working hands.

HELEN

How old were you when he died?

MATT

Fourteen.

HELEN

Hmm.

Matt exhales cigarette smoke and looks at Helen.

MATT

Why's you a nun?

HELEN

I was drawn to it, I guess. I mean, that's a hard question to answer. It's like asking you why you're a convict.

MATT

Bad luck.

HELEN

Good luck, then. I had a loving family, a lot of support. I guess I felt obliged to give some of it back.

MATT

Don't you miss havin' a man? Don't you want to get married, fall in love, have sex?

Helen looks at Matt.

What, you don't want to talk about it?

HELEN

Well, I have close friends, men and women. I've never experienced sexual intimacy, but there's other ways of being close. Sharing you dreams, your thoughts, your feelings.

Matt looks at Helen. The mesh screen has gone from the image.

That's bein' intimate, too.

MATT

We got intimacy right now, don't we, Sister?

Helen looks at Matt.

HELEN

I went to see your mother. She said she'd appear at the pardon board hearing if you want her to.

MATT

I like being alone with you. You're looking real good to me.

HELEN

Look at you. Death is breathing down your neck and you're playing your little Matt-on-the-make games.

Matt looks at Helen.

I'm not here for your amusement, Matthew. Show some respect.

MATT

Why should I respect you? 'Cause you're a nun? 'Cause you wear a little cross around your neck?

HELEN

Because I'm a person. Every person deserves respect.

Matt looks at Helen. He takes a drag from his cigarette.

What's the answer, what's it gonna be with your mama?

LUCILLE

(*voice-over*)

Mattie had a hard life, but he was a good boy.

INT. PARDON BOARD HEARING ROOM. DAY

Lucille sits at the defendant's table. An attorney sits to the right of her. Matt sits to the left of her. Hilton sits to the right of Matt and looks at Lucille. Helen and Colleen sit behind the defendant's table.

LUCILLE

(*crying*)

When he was six, he . . .

Lucille drops her head to the table, sobbing.

Lucille is helped up by one of the attorneys and Helen. Hilton grabs the microphone and places it in front of him as Helen helps Lucille away.

HILTON

Ladies and gentlemen, let's be honest. You're not gonna find many rich people on Death Row. Matthew Poncelet's here today because he's poor. Didn't have money for representation, so he had to take what the state gave him. The state gave him a tax lawyer who never tried a capital case before. An amateur. The jury selection took four hours.

Four members of the review board listen.

The trial lasted five days.

Matt and Hilton sit at the defendant's table.

The lawyer raised one objection the entire trial. Now, if Matthew had himself some money, well, he could have hired a team of crackerjack lawyers and they would have hired top-notch investigators, a ballistics expert, a psychologist to compile profiles of desirable jurors and you can be sure Matthew Poncelet wouldn't be sitting here today, before you, asking for his life.

Members of the review board listen intently.

Hilton stands.

The death penalty. It's nothing new, been with us for centuries.

EXT. OUTSIDE THE HEARING ROOM. DAY

Helen has her arm around Lucille, who is crying.

HILTON
(*voice-over*)

We've buried people alive, lopped off their heads with an axe, burned them alive in public squares, gruesome spectacles all.

Lucille looks at some snapshots she holds.

LUCILLE

I wanted them to see these pictures.

HILTON
(*voice-over*)

In . . .

Lucille is looking through some snapshots of Matt as a child.

. . . this century we kept searching for more and more humane ways . . .

Lucille is comforted by Helen.

. . . of killing people that we didn't like. We've shot 'em with firing squads, suffocated them in the gas chamber . . .

INT. PARDON BOARD HEARING ROOM. DAY

Hilton walks to the microphone.

HILTON

. . . but now, now we have developed a device that is the most humane of all: lethal injection. We strap the guy up, we anesthetize him with shot number one. Then we give him shot number two that implodes his lungs and shot number three stops his heart. We put him to death just like an old horse. His face just goes to sleep, while inside, his organs are going through Armageddon.

Helen enters and sits down.

(*off*)

The muscles of his face would twist and contort and . . .

Matt glances over his shoulder at Helen. Hilton speaks to the review board.

(*on screen*)

. . . pull, but you see, shot number one relaxes all . . .

Helen smiles at Matt.

. . . those muscles, so we don't have to see any horror show. We don't have to taste the blood of revenge on our lips, while this human being's organs writhe, twist, contort. We just sit there quietly, nod our heads, and say, 'Justice has been done.'

The assistant DA, Guy Gilardi, speaks to the pardon board. One member looks through pictures of the murder victims.

GILARDI

(*voice-over*)

It has been six . . .

A small TV monitor sits on a table. Matt's image can be seen on it.

. . . years since the brutal and reprehensible . . .

Helen listens.

. . . murders of Hope Percy and Walter Delacroix. Justice is long past due. Matt Poncelet has had a lengthy, thorough court review, not only at trial, but a retrial for sentencing as well as numerous appeals to State and Federal Courts and successive petitions filed by Mr Barber. There has been no doubt in the court's mind at any time about who did the murder.

Gilardi leans over the table and looks at two review board members.

Matthew Poncelet is not a good boy.

Helen listens.

(*off*)

He is a heartless killer. These murders . . .

A board member (arms only) looks through pictures of the murder victims.

. . . were calculated, disgusting and cruel.

Gilardi points at Matt, who sits beside Hilton.

This man shot Walter Delacroix two times in the back of his head.

We see Matt's face.

And raped Hope Percy and stabbed her seventeen times before shooting this sweet girl two times in the back of the head.

Gilardi walks toward the courtroom audience.

These families . . .

Mr Clyde and Mrs Mary Beth Percy, Hope's parents, are listening to Gilardi.

. . . will never see their children graduate from college. They will . . .

Helen looks past Colleen to the Percys.

. . . never attend their weddings.

Helen glances over her shoulder at the other victim's parents, Mr and Mrs Delacroix.

They will never have Christmas with them again. There will be no grandchildren. All they ask of you is simple justice for their unbearable loss.

Gilardi sits at the prosecution table speaking to the review board. One member sits looking through pictures of the murder victims.

I ask you to take a breath, steel your spine and proceed with the execution of Matthew Poncelet.

INT. PARDON BOARD BUILDING. DAY

Helen and Hilton are walking.

HILTON

It's always a good sign when you have to wait. I don't know whether we made any headway in there.

HELEN

I thought you did great.

HILTON

The best thing would be if they realized their own culpability in the death of a man.

Henry enters and approaches Hilton.

HENRY

Hilton.

HILTON

Hmm?

Henry gestures for Hilton to come with him.

Excuse me, Sister.

Henry and Hilton walk away. Helen walks on. Mr Delacroix walks toward her. Mrs Delacroix stands behind him.

MR DELACROIX

I'm Walter Delacroix's father.

Helen looks at Mr Delacroix.

HELEN

Mr Delacroix, I'm sorry about your son.

MR DELACROIX

(*interrupting*)

Sister, I'm a Catholic. How can you sit by Poncelet's side without ever having come to visit with me and my wife or the Percys to hear our side? How can you spend all your time worrying about Poncelet and not think that maybe we needed you too?

HELEN

Mr Delacroix, I didn't think . . .

Mr Delacroix looks at Helen. Mr and Mrs Percy step in and stand behind Mr Delacroix.

. . . that you wanted to talk to me.

Clyde Percy taps Mr Delacroix on the shoulder. Mr Delacroix looks at him.

CLYDE

Earl, we're goin' in.

Mr Delacroix looks at Helen.

MR DELACROIX

This is Mary Beth and Clyde Percy.

HELEN

I'm sorry about your daughter.

CLYDE

Yeah, so are we. Excuse us.

The Percys start to walk away.

Helen looks at Mr Delacroix and at the Percys. Mr Delacroix steps towards her.

MR DELACROIX

Listen, Sister, I'm sure you've seen a side of Matt Poncelet that none of us has seen. I'm sure he's on his best behavior, must be pretty sympathetic to ya, but, Sister, this is an evil man. This is a man who abducted teenage kids and raped and killed them. That scum robbed me of my only son. My name . . . my family name dies with me. There will be no more Delacroixs, Sister. No more.

HELEN

I want you to know I do care about you and your family, and what happened to your son.

Helen looks down into her purse.

I'm gonna give you my number and if there's anything that you need, you just call me.

Mr Delacroix looks down at Helen.

MR DELACROIX

Me call you?

Helen looks up at Mr Delacroix.

Think about that, Sister. Think about how arrogant that is. Excuse me.

As Mr Delacroix walks away, the camera reveals Hilton standing beside Helen. He looks down at her.

HILTON

You all right?

Helen looks down, hurt.

HILTON

We better be gettin' on in.

Helen walks towards the building. Hilton follows.

INT. PARDON BOARD HEARING ROOM. DAY

The pardon board members walk in a single file.

Helen looks at the board members.

Out in the hallway, Lucille enters and looks in through the hearing room window.

Hilton and Matt look at the board members, who sit down at the table. Mirabeau speaks.

MIRABEAU

(*off*)

It is the finding of this board that clemency be denied to Matthew Poncelet. Execution will . . .

Helen looks shocked.

. . . be carried out as scheduled one week hence.

Through the hearing room window Lucille sobs. Inside the hearing room, there are low murmers from the witnesses, reacting to the finding.

HILTON

(*off*)

Don't give up hope, Matt.

MIRABEAU

(*off, overlapping*)

Please remain seated until the prisoner has been escorted from the room.

HILTON

(*off, overlapping*)

We still got a judge in the Fifth Circuit Federal Court that can put a stop to this. Beyond that . . .

Hilton looks at Matt. Two guards position themselves behind Matt, who starts to stand up.

. . . there's the US Supreme Court and the Governor. I'll get a private meeting with him if it's the last thing I do.

Matt turns and looks down at Helen as the two guards take him by the arms.

MATT

Looks like you're all I got, Sis. They tell me I can have a spiritual advisor of my choice. Will you do it?

Helen looks up at Matt (*torso only*).

Matt looks down at Helen as the two guards escort him out of room.

Ride along into the sunset with me.

Helen looks up at Matt. She stares, a shocked look on her face.

HILTON

(*voice-over*)

It means you're going to have to spend several hours with him every day as his death nears.

EXT. PARDON BOARD HEARING. DAY

Hilton looks at Helen as they slowly walk in a line toward a bus.

HILTON

And then on the day of his execution, you're gonna have to spend all day with him. It's not an easy job. Usually it's done by a chaplain or a priest or a Muslim cleric.

HELEN

(*low*)

It's all right.

HILTON

It's just that I want you to be realistic about this. We've got about a one in one thousand chance things might go our way. It's a tough road.

Helen disappears onto the bus. Hilton follows.

HELEN

(*voice-over*)

What you could . . .

INT. PREJEAN APARTMENT. NIGHT

Helen and a teenage boy, Herbie, play checkers. Three younger children, including Palmer and Kenitra, play cards.

HELEN

. . . do then, if that had been a king, you could have gone back over again, but . . .

HERBIE

(*overlapping, indistinct*)

. . . me to go there again?

HELEN

(*overlapping*)

. . . you can go either way. You can jump three this way, then you can go all the way back.

BOY I

Go ahead.

KENITRA

I'm looking for a four.

HERBIE

(*indistinct*)

. . . go.

PALMER

Let her go. She got that big old fat joker there and she don't want to put it down. That's a shame. Shame.

HERBIE

Shame, shame.

HELEN

(*overlapping*)

All right. My turn. My turn.

Palmer flicks a card. It lands in front of Helen and she picks it up.

I got an ace. (*Laughing.*) I'm really lucky. Whose was this?

Helen hands the card to Palmer.

PALMER

Mine.

HELEN

All right.

INT. HELEN'S CAR/EXT. SLIDELL STREET. DAY

Through the windshield. The car travels down the street. On the radio: Purvis Slade, a shock jock.

SLADE

(*over radio*)

Oh, please don't kill him. He's a child of God. He deserves more. He's reformed. He's a poet, blah, blah, blah. Attention all you folks, ye advocates of . . .

Through the windshield. Helen drives. Shadows of trees fall across her face.

. . . killers and child molesters, ye opponents of execution. Ye cannot walk upon the high ground. Ye do not have the moral authority to walk there. Ye traverse with scum and scum is where ye lay . . .

Helen (hand only) turns off the radio.

INT./EXT. DELACROIX HOUSE. DAY

Helen walks up to the door and rings the doorbell.

Helen faces the screen door.

Helen looks up as she hears a door open.

Mr Delacroix exits from the house and looks down at Helen.

MR DELACROIX

What do you want?

HELEN

Mr Delacroix, forgive me for intruding, but I haven't been able to get you and your wife out of my mind. I've been trying to call you, but there's been no answer. Can I please speak with you?

MR DELACROIX

Sure.

HELEN

I'm really, really sorry for not coming to visit with you and your wife before this, but I've never been involved in anything like this before.

MR DELACROIX

Truth is, you're scared.

HELEN

Yes.

MR DELACROIX

I'd be too.

Mr Delacroix opens the screen door and gestures with his head for Helen to come inside.

Come in.

Helen smiles at Mr Delacroix.

HELEN

Thank you.

Helen walks through the screen door and follows Mr Delacroix toward the front door.

INT. DELACROIX HOUSE. LIVING ROOM. DAY

Mr Delacroix enters.

MR DELACROIX

Well, Sister . . .

Helen enters and looks at Mr Delacroix.

. . . can I ask you a question?

Helen nods.

Are you a Communist?

HELEN

Communist? No.

Mr Delacroix picks up a box and some lampshades and sets them on another sofa.

MR DELACROIX

I didn't think so. That's what some people around here are saying with you defending this murderer, but I didn't think so. Sit down.

HELEN

Thank you.

Helen crosses to the sofa and sits down. Mr Delacroix looks down at her.

MR DELACROIX

Care for some coffee?

HELEN

Thank you.

Mr Delacroix walks toward the kitchen.

MR DELACROIX

(*off*)

Sorry about the mess. My wife and I had a big fight.

Helen looks at a photograph hanging on the wall of a young Mr and Mrs Delacroix. There is a photograph of their son, Walter, beside it.

We got back from the pardon board hearing. She . . .

Mr Delacroix carries a cup of coffee into the living room.

. . . took Walter's clothes out of his closet, put 'em in boxes, called Goodwill.

Mr Delacroix reaches for a chair.

Helen looks at Mr Delacroix, who carries a chair towards her.

(*off*)
She says she wants to put the past behind her. She says she . . .

Mr Delacroix hands the cup of coffee to Helen.

. . . has to move on in her life. She's not herself.

HELEN
It must be so hard.

MR DELACROIX
When it first happened, she would have me bring her to Walter's grave every morning. She wept a river, poor woman. Whole days, nights, for weeks, months. I wish there was some way, some key into the past to change it. It tears me up. She used to be a ball. We would have us some fun, boy.

Mr Delacroix smiles and reaches down. He laughs.

He reaches into a box and pulls out a framed picture. He laughs.

Some times. Laugh. Laugh our heads off.

Mr Delacroix turns the picture frame around to reveal a picture of Walter as a little boy.

Helen looks down at the picture.

Walter learned how to walk on this floor right here.

Helen looks up at Mr Delacroix.

He busted his chin on the arm of that sofa right there. On that loveseat right there he sat with Hope the week before they died. When you lose a child, all the memories get sealed in a place. Sealed. Like a . . . shrine.

INT. CHAPLAIN'S OFFICE. DAY

Helen sits, looking across the desk at Farley.

FARLEY

So, you've put in a request to be the spiritual advisor to Matthew Poncelet.

HELEN

Yes, Father.

FARLEY

Why?

HELEN

He asked me.

Farley looks at Helen.

FARLEY

This is highly unusual.

HELEN

Why?

FARLEY

Well, you would be the first woman to do it.

HELEN

Really?

FARLEY

This kind of situation requires an experienced hand. This boy is to be executed in six days and is in dire need of redemption.

Helen swallows hard.

Are you up to this?

HELEN

I don't know, Father. I hope so. I've been praying for guidance.

FARLEY

You can save this boy by getting him to receive the sacraments of the Church before he dies. This is your job. Nothing more, nothing less. If you need any help, please feel free to call on me.

HELEN

Thank you, Father.

INT. DEATH ROW. DAY

Helen looks through the mesh screen at Matt.

MATT

I don't wanna be buried here. They said they was gonna call my mama, ask her about the funeral and all the arrangements. If you don't mind, could you do that? My mama'd fall apart on 'em.

HELEN

I'll do it. You ever read the Bible?

MATT

Yes, ma'am. I mean, I ain't much of a Bible reader, but I pick it up from time to time.

HELEN

Like W. C. Fields read his Bible?

MATT

Who?

HELEN

W. C. Fields. He used to play this drunken character in the movies. So he's on his death bed and a friend comes to visit and he sees him reading the Bible. The friend says, 'W. C., you don't believe in God, what are you doing reading the Bible?' And Fields says, 'I'm lookin' for a loophole.'

Matt smiles.

Helen looks through the mesh screen at Matt, who looks away.

MATT

I ain't lookin' for no loophole. Rain, rain, rain.

Matt puts a cigarette in his mouth.

That's a bad sign. They already executed one black, Tobias; Wayne Purcell tonight. That's two blacks.

Matt lights his cigarette.

Time for a white. The Governor's under pressure to get a white. And that's me.

Helen looks at Matt.

Nigger on the gurney before me. I sure hope they clean that thing before they put me on it.

HELEN

Was your daddy a racist?

Matt smokes and looks at Helen.

MATT

What kind of question is that?

HELEN

You have to teach a child to hate, and I was just wondering who taught you.

MATT

I just don't like niggers.

HELEN

Have you ever known any black people?

MATT

Sure I did. They was all around when I was a kid.

HELEN

All around?

MATT

Yeah. Lived around me.

HELEN

Did you ever play with a black child?

MATT

No. But me and my cousin got jumped pretty good once.

HELEN

What happened?

MATT

We was throwing rocks at 'em. So the next day, they wait their chance, get a hold of our bikes, tear 'em up.

HELEN

Can you blame 'em?

MATT

Well, no, but look, slavery's long over. They're always harping on what a bad deal they got.

HELEN

The kids that tore up your bike?

MATT

All of 'em. I can't stand people who make themselves out to be victims.

HELEN

Victims.

MATT

Yeah, they all victims.

HELEN

I don't know any victims in my neighborhood. I know some pretty cool people, decent, hard-working.

MATT

Yeah, I know a lot of lazy, welfare-taking coloreds sucking up tax dollars.

HELEN

You sound like a politician.

MATT

What's that mean?

HELEN

You ever been the object of prejudice?

Matt shakes his head.

MATT

No.

Helen looks at Matt.

HELEN

What do you suppose people think about inmates on Death Row?

MATT

I don't know, why don't you tell me?

HELEN

They're all monsters. Disposable human waste, good-for-nothings sucking up tax dollars.

MATT

Yeah, well, I ain't no victim. They're gonna kill me, I'm innocent. I ain't whining. I ain't sittin' on no porch going 'slavery, slavery'. I like rebels, some blacks is okay. Martin Luther King, he led his people all the way to DC, kicked the white man's butt.

HELEN

You respect Martin Luther King?

MATT

Well, he put up a fight, he wasn't lazy.

HELEN

What about lazy whites?

MATT

Don't like 'em.

HELEN

So it's lazy people you don't like.

MATT

Can we talk about something else?

HELEN

Yeah.

Matt takes a drag of cigarette.

EXT. ANGOLA PRISON GATE. NIGHT

A group of demonstrators stand outside the gate. Some hold signs that read:

AN EYE FOR AN EYE	KILL A KILLER	REVENGE IS SWEET

Low, overlapping chatter continues under the following scenes.

Clyde and Mary Beth Percy stand among the group of demonstrators.

Mr Delacroix stands among the group of demonstrators. Helen is standing in a circle with another group of demonstrators, holding a candlelight vigil.

SUPPORTER

Jesus also said, 'He who lives by the sword shall die by the sword.' Purcell had it coming to him. Do you understand? He had it coming!

SUPPORTERS

(*counting down*)

Nine, eight, seven, six, five, four, three, two, one.

Overlapping cheers.

Yay!!! Yay!!! Whooo!

Clyde and Mary Beth Percy are being interviewed by a TV crew. A pick-up truck crosses in the background. Two guards are inside. One is Sergeant Neil Trapp.

CLYDE

It's the only way we can be sure that they will not kill again. Life without parole, oh sure. How many prison guards? How many other prisoners do they have to kill before it's over? These people are mad dogs. Maniacs.

Helen looks around. Colleen is behind.

COLLEEN

Come on. Let's go.

Helen walks away, touching a man on the shoulder.

HELEN

Bye.

MAN

Bye.

INT. HELEN'S CAR. NIGHT

Helen drives. Colleen sits beside her.

HELEN

If the Governor and the courts turn us down, Matt's gonna be dead in six days.

Colleen shakes her head.

COLLEEN

Mmmm.

HELEN

We gotta get us a funeral home and some place to bury him.

COLLEEN

Maybe our sisters will donate one of their burial plots.

HELEN

Somebody to do the burial service. Clothes. I, I guess . . . a suit.

COLLEEN

Suit? What size suit do you think he wears?

HELEN

I don't know.

COLLEEN

How tall is he?

Helen looks at Colleen.

HELEN

I don't know. I think he's kinda big. What size is kinda big? Does it run like big, medium and petite?

Colleen laughs.

Helen and Colleen laugh.

Well, I don't know. I never bought a man's suit before.

COLLEEN

Wouldn't you be a pretty sight? A nun shopping for a man's suit.

They laugh.

HELEN

Oh, I'm out of my league. This is so surreal.

INT. PERCY HOUSE. DAY

The camera pans over pictures of Hope and the rest of the Percy family, and tilts down to Clyde and Mary Beth Percy, who sit on the sofa.

MARY BETH

(*off*)

Hope had just graduated from high school in early May. She was to join the Air Force on June fifteenth. That's the day it happened. She almost got out of Slidell.

CLYDE

She was hopin' to get stationed overseas.

Helen sits in a chair looking at the Percys.

(*off*)

She liked to travel and loved being around people of different cultures.

MARY BETH

June fifteenth, a recruiting sergeant was to meet her up in Slidell and drive her to Baton Rouge for induction. The day before, I took her shopping for things she'd need, you know, just practical things, and . . .

CLYDE

. . . that evening about five o'clock she got dressed and headed off to work over at Corey's, where she waitressed. After work she had a date with Walter.

MARY BETH

When she was about to leave, I . . . the hem of her skirt was coming out and I . . . She was in such a hurry, so . . .

FLASHBACK – INT. COURTROOM. DAY

Gilardi (hands only) reaches into the bag marked 'evidence' and pulls out Hope's safety-pinned skirt. Gilardi shows the skirt to Mary Beth, who is on the witness stand.

MARY BETH

(*voice-over*)

. . . I pinned it for her with one of those little tiny safety pins. She was gone out the door. You don't know when you see your child leave through a door that you're never gonna see them alive again.

INT. PERCY HOUSE. DAY

Clyde and Mary Beth look at Helen. Mary Beth speaks through tears.

MARY BETH

If I'd known that, I would have told her how much I love her. You know my last words to her, the last that she ever heard from me, were about the hem of a skirt.

Helen's eyes fill with tears as she listens.

CLYDE

(*off*)

Next morning we waited for her to come out of that door.

(*sighs*)

This was Hope's big day. Our baby was . . .

FLASHBACK – INT. HOPE'S BEDROOM. DAY

The door opens. There is an empty, neatly made bed.

CLYDE

(*voice-over*)

. . . leaving home.

MARY BETH

(*voice-over*)

Her room was empty and the bed was still neatly made.

INT. PERCY HOUSE. DAY

Helen listens, tears in her eyes.

MARY BETH

So I telephoned the Delacroixs and . . .

CLYDE

Our hearts sank when the Delacroixs told us that Walter hadn't come home that night too. And then for one brief moment we thought, well . . . maybe they'd run off and gotten married or something.

Helen listens.

MARY BETH

But we knew that she was just too sensible a girl to do somethin' like that.

CLYDE

I went down to the police and . . . filled out a Missing Person's form.

Mary Beth sniffles while he speaks.

FLASHBACK – EXT. LOUISIANA WOODS. DAY

A search party walks through the tall weeds. Clyde is among them.

CLYDE

(*voice-over*)

Three days later the sheriff formed a search party and I went along with 'em.

MARY BETH

(*voice-over*)

They were gone all day, they just walked for miles and nothin'.

INT. PERCY HOUSE. DAY

Clyde and Mary Beth sit on the sofa looking at Helen.

CLYDE

On Thursday 20 June some kids were walking near Flank's Cove and they found a . . .

Mary Beth is trying to hold back tears.

. . . purse and some clothing and . . . and a wallet. And they turned them in to the police.

Helen looks at Clyde, tears in her eyes.

They found the kids' bodies on Friday, six days after they'd gone missing.

FLASHBACK – EXT. FLANK'S COVE. TWILIGHT

Two sheriff's deputies look down at the two lifeless bodies.

MARY BETH
(*voice-over*)
My daughter's body was nude, legs spread-eagle. Coroner's report said that . . .

INT. PERCY HOUSE. DAY

Clyde and Mary Beth.

MARY BETH
. . . her vagina was all tore up.

Helen listens, tears in her eyes.

At first they couldn't find this, well, class pin that she was wearing 'cause it was embedded so deep, from the stabbin'. She loved that pin. She was so proud of it. She wore it all the time. It said: 'Class of '88 making a difference.'

CLYDE
The police wouldn't let us go down to the morgue and identify the body. They said it would be too traumatic.

MARY BETH
I just couldn't bear the thought of them burying that body without making absolutely and positively sure that that was Hope. So I called my brother, he's a dentist, and I asked him to go over to the funeral home and make an ID from dental records.

CLYDE
Before he'd stuck his hand into that bag with all that lime in it and fished Hope's jaw out, he'd been against the death penalty. But after that, he was all for it.

MARY BETH
I knew it had to be Hope. That's what my mind told me, you know, but I just . . . I had to be sure.

Helen looks up at Emily, Hope's fourteen-year-old sister.

Clyde and Mary Beth look at Emily.

Emily looks around and walks toward her parents.

Mary Beth sniffles.

Helen wipes the tears from her face.

Clyde wipes his eyes. Emily whispers into Mary Beth's ear.

EMILY

Can I watch TV?

MARY BETH

All right, Emily. This is Sister Helen Prejean.

Emily looks smugly at Helen.

EMILY

Hello.

Helen nods at Emily.

HELEN

Nice to meet you, Emily.

Emily bends over Mary Beth.

EMILY

Okay?

Emily stands up.

MARY BETH

Okay. Let's go in the kitchen, I'll make us some coffee.

Mary Beth exits, followed by Helen and Clyde. Emily turns on the TV.

FLASHBACK – INT. COURTROOM/HALLWAY. DAY

Two guards are leading Matt out of the courtroom. Matt walks past Clyde, who looks at him.

CLYDE
(*voice-over*)
I met Poncelet face to face in the hallway during the trial.

MATT
I ain't gonna get no chair, Daddy.

CLYDE
You're gonna fry. And I'm gonna watch you sizzle.

Matt is led toward a door.

MATT
Whoo!

The camera tilts down to a sheriff's holster gun, Clyde's hand next to it.

CLYDE
(*voice-over*)
There was a sheriff standing pretty close by me. I could have grabbed his gun, I could have shot Poncelet right then and there.

INT. PERCY LIVING ROOM. DAY

Emily sits on the sofa listening to Clyde talking in the kitchen.

CLYDE
(*voice-over*)
I coulda killed him on that day.

Emily looks at the TV.

And I wished I would have.

INT. PERCY KITCHEN. DAY

Helen sits at the table with Clyde and Mary Beth.

CLYDE
I'd be a happier man today.

Mary Beth looks at Helen.

MARY BETH
So, what made you change your mind?

Helen looks confused.

HELEN

Change my mind?

MARY BETH

What made you come round to our side?

Helen looks caught off guard.

HELEN

Well, I . . . I just, I wanted to come and see if I could help y'all and . . .

Mary Beth nods.

. . . pray with you.

MARY BETH

Thank you.

HELEN

But . . . he asked me to be his spiritual advisor, to be with him when he dies.

MARY BETH

And what did you say?

HELEN

That I would.

Clyde looks stunned.

CLYDE

We thought you'd changed your mind. We thought that's why you were here.

Helen shakes her head.

HELEN

No.

MARY BETH

How can you come here?

CLYDE

How can you do that? How can you sit with that scum?

HELEN

Mr Percy, I, I've never done this before. I'm tryin', I'm just tryin' to follow the example of Jesus. Who said that every person is worth more than their worst act.

CLYDE

This is not a person. This is an animal. No, I take that back. Animals don't rape and murder their own kind. Matthew Poncelet is God's mistake. And you want to hold the poor murderer's hand? You want to be there to comfort him when he dies? There wasn't anybody in the woods that night to comfort Hope when those two animals pushed her face down in the wet grass.

HELEN

Sir. I just want to help him take responsibility for what he did.

Mary Beth looks at Helen, tears in her eyes.

MARY BETH

Does he admit to what he did? Is he sorry?

HELEN

He says he didn't kill anybody.

CLYDE

Sister, you're in waters way over your head.

MARY BETH

You don't know what it's like to carry a child in your womb and give birth and get up with a sick child in the middle of the night. You just say your prayers and get a good night's sleep, don't you?

CLYDE

I'm trying to be respectful. My parents raised me to respect the religious. Sister, I think you need to leave this house right now.

HELEN

I'm sorry.

Helen rises and starts to leave.

CLYDE

Wait a minute!

Clyde stands.

Helen stops, facing the door.

If you really are sorry . . .

Helen turns around.

. . . and you . . .

Clyde walks toward Helen. Mary Beth is behind him.

. . . really do care about this family, you'll want to see justice done for our murdered child.

Helen looks at Clyde, tears in her eyes.

Now, you can't have it both ways. You can't befriend that murderer and expect to be our friend too.

MARY BETH

You brought the enemy into this house, Sister. You better go.

INT. HELEN'S CAR. DAY

Helen drives, tears streaming down her cheek.

INT. PREJEAN APARTMENT. NIGHT

Matt is being interviewed on TV. The caption reads: 'MATTHEW PONCELET: CONDEMNED INMATE'.

MATT

(*on screen*)

I come from a good family. My family can't be blamed for nothin'. I had two families. Both of 'em I'd live and die for.

REPORTER

Your other family is . . .

MATT

The family of Man. Of men in prison. My white family, the Aryan Brotherhood.

Helen sits in a chair looking at the TV. Colleen stands beside her, also watching the TV.

REPORTER

You're a white supremacist? A follower of Hitler?

MATT

Hitler was a leader. I admire him for getting things done. It's like Castro, now, he got things done, man. I mean, Hitler might have gone overboard on the killing and stuff but he was on the right track that the Aryan was the master race.

REPORTER

The right track? The murder of six million Jews?

MATT

That's never been proven. Your government's been doing plenty of evil things themselves and you're paying for it . . .

HELEN

What am I doing with this guy? I must be nuts.

MATT

. . . took part in the political assassination of Castro, Allende, the Sandinistas.

The phone rings. Helen answers it.

The government shouldn't have the power to execute nobody.

HELEN

(*into telephone*)

Hello?

HILTON

(*over telephone*)

Sister? It's Hilton Barber. We need you to come in for a strategy meeting.

INT. HILTON BARBER'S OFFICE. DAY

Hilton's staff buzz about the office. Some of the staff sit around a table. Hilton's associate Nellie looks down at a newspaper clipping she is holding.

NELLIE

In an interview with the *Shreveport Times*, Poncelet says that if he had to do it all over again, he would do something useful like join a terrorist group and bomb government buildings. We've got to get him off this political prisoner kick.

Hilton is sitting at a desk looking up at his associate Henry, who searches through some files that sit on the desk.

HILTON

Henry, how close are we on the Supreme Court docket?

HENRY

Oh, in a couple of days.

HILTON

Couple of days? We don't have a couple of days!

HENRY

Yeah, well, we don't have the legal staff, Hilton.

HILTON

You've had it for three days. Where were you yesterday, anyway?

Henry takes a document from the files, walks back and sits down as Hilton stands up.

HENRY

I had to take my kid to the dentist.

Hilton walks past Henry.

HILTON

A man is gonna die on Death Row and you're off gallivanting . . .

HENRY

Yeah, well, my kid needed to hold her daddy's hand.

HILTON

What?

HENRY

If you don't like it, find another lawyer to volunteer his time.

The camera pans up off Henry on to Helen, who stares out of the window.

Through the window, three slackers hang out on a doorstep.

HELEN
(*voice-over*)
People are reading these interviews, thinking . . .

INT. DEATH HOUSE. DAY

Matt looks through the mesh screen at Helen, who paces, holding some papers.

. . . you're some kind of a nut: admiring Hitler, wanting to come back as a terrorist and blow people up.

Helen slams the papers down in front of the mesh screen and walks away.

MATT
I didn't say nothin' about people. Buildings, government buildings, not people.

HELEN
How can you bomb a building without hurtin' somebody?

MATT
Hey, I ain't got no love for the US government, alright?

HELEN
You're a fool. You are makin' it so easy for them to kill you, coming across as some kind of a crazed animal, Nazi, racist mad dog who deserves to die.

MATT
Is that what you think?

Helen looks at Matt.

HELEN
You are making it so difficult to help you.

Matt looks at Helen.

MATT
You can leave.

HELEN

I'm not gonna do that.

Matt looks at Helen and turns away.

It's up to you. You want me to go, you say so.

Matt looks at Helen.

Do you ever think about those kids?

Matt shakes his head.

MATT

Hey, it's terrible what happened to them kids.

HELEN

Especially since it didn't have to happen. What about their parents? Do you ever think about what you and Vitello did to their parents' lives?

MATT

It's hard, ma'am, to have much sympathy for them parents when, here, they're trying to kill me.

HELEN

Well, think about it. Their kids are shot, stabbed, raped, left in the woods to die alone. How would you feel if somebody did that to your mama, or your little brother? What would you want to do to them?

MATT

I'd kill 'em. I'd sure as hell want to kill them. I understand them parents calling for blood, but they're callin' for the wrong head. I want to take a lie detector test.

HELEN

What?

MATT

A lie detector test. I know it ain't gonna change them guys' minds, but I want my mama to know the truth. I want my mama to know I didn't kill them kids.

Helen looks at Matt, stunned.

Matt looks at Helen and walks away.

INT. PREJEAN APARTMENT. DAY

Colleen sits on the couch looking down at the three children, Kenitra, Herbie and Palmer, who play a board game.

COLLEEN

That was good. Go.

Helen enters.

HELEN

Hey, y'all.

COLLEEN

Hey.

Helen walks toward the kids.

HELEN

Havin' a party, Palmer?

Helen squats down beside Kenitra and looks at Herbie.

Herbie, how's your side feeling?

HERBIE

Okay.

Herbie and Palmer exit. Helen looks at Kenitra.

HELEN

Kenitra, how are you doing?

KENITRA

Fine.

Herbie looks back at Kenitra.

HERBIE

Come on, Kenitra, let's go.

Kenitra gets up and follows Herbie and Palmer towards the door.

COLLEEN

Bye, bye.

Helen glances at Colleen, confused.

HELEN

Wait a minute, what happened?

COLLEEN

There's talk in the neighborhood. Someone read some of Poncelet's racist comments. Your name was in the article.

HELEN

Oh, Lord.

COLLEEN

They're also wondering where you've been at the learning center. Think you care more about him than your classes.

HELEN

Colleen, I'm so . . .

Helen reaches for Colleen's hand.

Colleen looks at Helen, and pats her hand.

. . . sorry.

COLLEEN

It's all right. I still love ya. I just thought you should know.

Colleen looks at Helen, then notices something.

Oh!

Colleen walks over and takes a suit from the coat rack.

Got this at Goodwill.

Helen walks toward her, and takes the suit.

I talked to Bishop Norwich. He said he would say the . . . funeral mass.

Helen sits in a chair. Colleen sits on the sofa and looks at her.

I also found a funeral home willing to donate their services. The leaders of the congregation met and we can use one of our own burial plots. If Matt dies, guess who he'll be buried next to.

HELEN

Who was the last person to die?

COLLEEN

Sister Celestine.

Helen puts her hand to her mouth, shocked.

HELEN

Oh, Lord.

COLLEEN

Remember when that sweet little girl came to the convent after her wedding to introduce her husband to us?

Helen cringes and looks at Colleen.

HELEN

And Sister Celestine said, 'I'm glad I'll never have to share my bed with a man.'

COLLEEN

She loved her celibacy so much.

HELEN

I know. She's gonna be lying next to a man for all eternity.

Colleen nods. The two break out in laughter.

INT. MEETING ROOM. NIGHT.

A victim support meeting is in progress. Camera pans around the circle of victim's family members to reveal Helen sitting next to Mr Delacroix.

MOTHER

My daughter's killer can possibly get out on parole in another year. He's only served six . . .

MAN

Recently, my wife and I went to the sheriff's office . . .

MOTHER

I just can't bear the thought of him being out a free man, and her buried in the ground and dead forever.

MAN

. . . to apply for victim compensation funds. The deputy rifled through a few drawers, 'Don't know nothin' about these files.'

WOMAN 2

. . . was killed by her ex-husband, you know. Stabbed to death in our backyard by my son's best friend. He'd spent the night at our house and gone to church with us that very morning.

MAN

I've just lost my job.

WOMAN 2

Her little skiing outfit is still in the closet.

MAN

I just couldn't pull it together . . .

WOMAN 3

When our child was killed, it took over a week to find her body.

MAN

. . . staring out the window. Couldn't concentrate.

WOMAN 3

The DA's office treated us like *we* were the criminals.

Helen looks at Mr Delacroix.

MR DELACROIX

My wife filed for divorce this afternoon. We just have different ways of dealing with our son's death. 'Until death do us part.'

EXT. SCHOOL. NIGHT

The door opens, and Helen steps out. She holds the door for Mr Delacroix.

MR DELACROIX

We're nothin' special.

Mr Delacroix steps out. The two walk on.

Most folks that lose a kid split up. Seventy per cent or something. I just wish I could laugh, find something funny. This is my car.

They stop at Mr Delacroix's car. Helen looks at him.

HELEN

Thanks for inviting me, Mr Delacroix.

MR DELACROIX

You take care, Sister.

HELEN

Good night.

Mr Delacroix opens the car door and gets in.

FLASHBACK – EXT. LOUISIANA WOODS. NIGHT

The camera dollies in towards a car parked in the woods.

Matt pushes Walter against the car, camera pulls back and tilts down to Hope's handcuffed hands.

INT. PRISON VEHICLE. DAY

We see Helen's face. Out of the window, prisoners work in the fields. Trapp is driving the car.

The car travels past a church and a man on a horse.

FLASHBACK – EXT. LOUISIANA WOODS. NIGHT

The camera dollies from behind a tree to reveal Matt looking down as Vitello stands over Hope, tearing off Hope's clothes.

IMAGINING

Part of a graduation picture (Hope only).

A picture of Walter and Hope in their graduation hats.

Part of a graduation picture (Walter only).

FLASHBACK – EXT. LOUISIANA WOODS. NIGHT

Matt (legs only) holds down Walter with his foot, and points a shotgun down at him. Camera tilts up to Matt's face.

IMAGINING

A formal picture of Hope and Walter.

A framed picture of Walter and Hope sits on a table.

FLASHBACK – LOUISIANA WOODS. NIGHT

The camera dollies from behind a tree and pans with Matt, who walks to the right. He looks back at Vitello.

MATT

What the fuck are you doing? Whatcha doin'?

Vitello enters and grabs the shotgun from Matt. Vitello points the gun down at Walter.

Matt backs away. A gunshot is heard.

The camera pans to Matt, who looks down at Walter. Matt backs away as another shot is heard.

Vitello looks down at Walter. Matt walks to the right and looks down at Walter.

IMAGINING

Close on a picture of Walter as a baby.

Close on a picture of Walter as a child.

Close on a picture of a young Walter.

Close on a picture of Walter as a baby (mouth and nose only).

Close on a picture of Walter as a child (eyes and nose only).

Close on a picture of Walter as a child.

INT. PRISON VEHICLE. DAY

Helen's POV. Out of the window. The car travels past a graveyard.

We see Helen's face.

INT. DEATH HOUSE. OFFICE. DAY

Beliveau sits at his desk. Helen enters in the outside hallway escorted by Trapp.

GUARD

Raise your arms.

Trapp looks at Helen, who raises her arms. One guard scans her with a metal detector. Another looks through her purse.

Go ahead.

Helen and Trapp walk on. Then Trapp points down the hallway to a chair.

TRAPP

Have a seat in that chair right there.

Helen walks and sits on the chair.

INT. DEATH HOUSE. HALLWAY. DAY

Through the window. The top half of the door opens. Matt is led by a guard, who sits him down in a chair.

Matt scoots the chair forward as the guard exits down the hallway.

Matt looks around through the window to Helen sitting on a chair. She looks at Matt.

MATT

Like my new digs?

HELEN

Heh. Hi.

Helen gets up and pulls her chair closer to the window. Matt looks through the glass at her.

MATT

I'm pretty special, huh?

Helen put her ear closer to the glass.

HELEN

What?

MATT

I'm pretty special . . . have this place all to myself. They got like ten guards guarding me. Got one guy that comes down every fifteen minutes just to see if I killed myself. Suicide watch.

Helen leans in to hear better.

Suicide watch. Never had so many people caring about what I was doin'.

HELEN

When did they bring you here?

MATT

Last night. Late. Didn't get to say goodbye to most of the guys on the Row, mostly they were sleepin'.

HELEN

Oh.

MATT

Did you take care of that, uh, lie detector test yet?

HELEN

I made some calls, but I haven't had any luck yet.

MATT

So this is the end, huh? My death house vacation. Three days of quiet. Plenty of time to read my Bible. Look for a loophole.

Helen didn't hear him. She puts her ear up to the window.

HELEN

Hmm?

MATT

Look for a loophole.

Helen smiles.

Matt looks through the window at Helen.

HELEN

Did you read anything about Jesus in that Bible?

MATT

Oh, Holy Man, did good, in Heaven. Praise Jesus.

HELEN

There are some passages in there about when Jesus was facing death alone that you might wanna check out.

MATT

Ah, I think me and Jesus have a different way of dealing with things. He's one of them turn the other cheek guys.

Through the window, Helen smiles at Matt.

HELEN

It takes a lot of strength to turn the other cheek. You, you say you like rebels. What do you think Jesus was?

MATT

He wasn't no rebel.

HELEN

Sure he was. He was a dangerous man.

MATT

What's so dangerous about love your brother?

HELEN

His love changed things.

Matt leans forward toward the window.

His love changed things. All those people nobody cared about, the prostitutes, the beggars, the poor. They finally had somebody who respected them, loved them, made 'em realize their own worth. They had dignity and they were becoming so powerful that the guys on the top got real nervous and so they had to kill Jesus.

MATT

Kinda like me, huh?

Helen is taken aback.

HELEN

Oh, Matt, not . . . not at all like you. Jesus changed the world with his love. You watched while two kids were murdered.

Matt and Helen look at each other. A buzzer is heard.

BELIVEAU
(*off*)

Step back from the door . . .

Helen looks up at Beliveau. Beliveau walks toward her as she stands.

. . . Sister.

Through the window, a guard walks toward Matt, and lifts him up from the chair.

HELEN
(*unseen, low*)

What's happening?

Through the office window, Beliveau unlocks the door. Other guards look on.

BELIVEAU

Move it on out, boy.

Matt walks out of the door, escorted by two guards.

MATT

Well, Sister . . . Um . . . What's this?

Beliveau walks past Helen, who looks off after Matt.

BELIVEAU

He'll be about an hour, Sister. Why don't you wait outside and get some air?

HELEN

Where are they takin' him?

BELIVEAU

I can't tell you.

Beliveau exits. Helen stares off, then turns and exits.

EXT. DEATH HOUSE/BENCH. DAY

Helen sits on a bench, staring off. A door opens and Trapp walks out. He looks at Helen.

TRAPP

Sister Helen? Chaplain Farley called. He's at the gate. He'll be right here.

HELEN

Thank you. Sergeant Trapp? How long do you think that big ole tree's been standing there?

Trapp looks up at a row of tall trees.

TRAPP

Well . . .

Trapp and Helen look off towards the trees.

. . . there ain't no telling.

Trapp starts to walk back towards the door, but stops and looks down at Helen as she speaks.

HELEN

Saw you outside the gates the other night at Purcell's execution.

TRAPP

Yeah?

HELEN

You seemed upset.

TRAPP

Upset? No.

Helen looks up at Trapp.

HELEN

Were you inside the room when they did it?

TRAPP

I'm on the strap down team. Left leg. That's my job. The left leg. We take the prisoner from his cell to the execution chamber.

HELEN

Wow. That's gotta be tough.

TRAPP

It's hard. I didn't sleep that night.

HELEN

I think it's gotta affect everybody that sees it, whether they're for it or against it.

TRAPP

It's just part of the job. These prisoners gets what's coming to 'em.

Trapp walks away.

FARLEY

(*voice-over*)

It's very easy for someone to come in here and make a . . .

INT. DEATH HOUSE OFFICE. DAY

Farley sits at his desk looking at Helen, who sits across from him.

FARLEY

. . . rash judgement on procedure. What may appear on the surface to be irrational or unnecessary proves upon examination to have solid reasoning and experience behind it.

HELEN

Father, all I'm asking is to play a hymn for Matt before his execution.

FARLEY

And experience tells us that music stirs up emotion.

Helen leans on the desk and looks at Farley.

Emotion that can produce an unexpected reaction in the inmate.

HELEN

All right. Do you have any objection to my asking the warden for his opinion.

Farley shakes his head.

FARLEY

I would oppose it, but you may if you like.

HELEN

Thank you. And thank you for your time.

Farley looks at Helen, who stands up.

FARLEY

I understand you were protesting outside the gates during the last execution.

HELEN

Yes.

FARLEY

Are you familiar with the Old Testament? 'Thou shalt not kill. But if anyone sheds the blood of man, then by man, shall his blood be shed.'

HELEN

Yes, Father. Are you familiar with the New Testament, where Jesus talks about grace and reconciliation?

FARLEY

Poncelet has to understand that Jesus died for his sins. If he accepts that reconciliation is his and his soul shall have eternal life. One's opinion of the death penalty is not the issue here. Look at

Romans. 'Let every person be subordinate to the higher authorities . . .'

As Farley speaks, camera moves in on his mouth.

'. . . There is no authority, except from God. And those who oppose it . . .'

Helen listens.

. . . will bring judgment upon themselves.'

Helen faints.

INT. PRISON HOSPITAL. CORRIDOR. DAY

The double doors burst open. Beliveau, Farley, a nurse and a guard push Helen on a stretcher. Another nurse enters and takes her place alongside the stretcher, helping them move it.

NURSE

What is it? What happened?

FARLEY

She collapsed in my office. I think it's her heart.

BELIVEAU

She's havin' a heart attack.

Helen sits up.

HELEN

I'm okay. I think I just fainted.

She lies back down.

BELIVEAU

No, no. Don't you move.

Helen tries to sit up.

HELEN

No, I'm hungry. I think I just need something to eat.

INT. PRISON HOSPITAL ROOM. DAY

Helen is lying in a hospital bed.

HELEN

I told Matt I'd be back. Could you tell him what happened, please?

NURSE

We'll do that when we're finished here.

HELEN

No, I really . . . I've gotta tell him now what happened.

FARLEY

I'll take care of it, Sister.

HELEN

Thank you.

NURSE

Well, good news, this isn't a heart attack.

Beliveau looks at Helen, who lies down looking up at the nurse. The nurse detaches the EKG monitors from Helen.

HELEN

I'm just hungry. They don't let visitors eat in the death house. They must think we're some kind of ferns that feed on air or somethin'.

The nurse looks down at Helen. She wraps a blood pressure belt around Helen's arm. Helen looks over at the EKG machine.

Is that the machine that they use after an execution?

NURSE

Yes, ma'am. Just have to be official about the whole thing.

Beliveau enters. The nurse replaces the blood pressure machine and looks down at Helen.

NURSE

Thank God we're off the electric chair. It's a little easier to take the needle. Just part of the job, you know. Let's get you up and get some food in your stomach.

HELEN

Who puts the needle in?

NURSE

That's private information.

HELEN

Is it you?

NURSE

We're not allowed to disclose any specifics regarding execution procedure.

BELIVEAU

Come on, Sister. Let me get you a tray of food and then we'll send you on home.

Helen sits up and buttons her shirt.

HELEN

I've gotta get back to Matt.

BELIVEAU

I'm sorry, Sister. Warden's orders, you're through for the day.

The nurse hands Helen her cross necklace.

INT. DEATH HOUSE. HALLWAY. DAY

A guard holds open the cell door as Matt walks out. He walks toward the window, looking through it at Helen, who sits there.

MATT

Where'd you go yesterday?

Helen stands. Matt walks towards her.

HELEN

They wouldn't let me come back.

MATT

You all right?

HELEN

Yeah, I'm fine. A lot of commotion for nothin'. I . . .

MATT

I kept askin' somebody what happened. Nobody'd tell me anything.

HELEN

What do you mean, you didn't know?

MATT

I thought you had a heart attack or somethin'.

HELEN

Man, they told me they were gonna tell you what happened. I . . .

MATT

And then they took me into that little room, wouldn't tell me why. They was . . .

Matt looks at Helen, whose reflection can be seen in the glass.

. . . weighin' me, measurin' me.

HELEN

Measuring you? What for?

MATT

Yeah. See how big a coffin I needed or somethin'.

HELEN

Oh . . .

MATT

Then I come back and you were gone. I spent the whole day alone.

HELEN

Oh, Matt, I'm sorry. I'm so sorry.

Matt sits down.

Helen looks at Matt, whose reflection can be seen in the window.

MATT

You ever get lonely?

HELEN

Yeah. Sure. Sometimes on Sundays when I smell the smoke from the neighborhood barbecues and I hear all the kids laughin' and I'm sittin' in my room, I feel like a fool.

MATT

Humph. What I miss most bein' here are women. Hmm. You know, I used to sit at the bar, just drinkin' and listenin' to music. I'd dance till three or four in the mornin'.

HELEN

Mmmm.

MATT

I ain't gonna lie, I believed in doin' it. Me and my lady friends, we'd grab a bottle, blanket, some weed, go out in the woods, and we'd do it. Umm. It's somethin' you've missed, ma'am.

HELEN

Well, let's face it, Matt, if I had a husband and a family, chances are I'd be with them right now instead of sitting here visiting with you.

MATT

Yeah, true enough. I'm glad you're here.

A pause.

HELEN

You want me to get a message to your daughter?

Matt rolls his eyes and looks at Helen.

MATT

Uhh . . . My . . . Let her be.

Helen nods. Matt puts a cigarette in his mouth.

HELEN

Those things'll kill ya.

Matt grunts, lights his cigarette and stands up.

MATT

I ain't gonna let 'em break me.

Matt walks off, looking back at Helen. A guard behind Matt stands.

I just pray God holds up my legs on my last walk. It's the wait, it's that countdown that gets to you.

HELEN

We're gonna know soon about the federal appeal. And Hilton and I, we got an appointment with the Governor this evening.

MATT

Fat chance the Governor's gonna do anything. Risk his political butt for me? Man, I wish I hadn't said all that shit about Hitler and bein' a terrorist. Stupid!

HELEN

Hartman says there won't be any more media interviews.

Matt sits back down, as does the guard.

MATT

(*sighs*)

Good. Keep my stupid mouth shut.

HELEN

I was able to arrange for a lie detector test for tomorrow morning.

MATT

All right. Well, there's some good news.

HELEN

Well, now, the man that's gonna be giving the test, he has serious doubts that they're gonna get an accurate readin' of the truth.

MATT

Why?

HELEN

Because tomorrow's the day of your execution. You're bound to be under stress and the test often mistakes stress for dishonesty.

MATT

No problem. I'm home free.

Helen nods.

HELEN

You been readin' your Bible?

MATT
(*sighs*)

I tried to last night.

Matt stands up. The guard behind him stands.

Makes me wanna sleep. I'm tryin' to stay conscious. I appreciate you tryin' to save me, but . . .

Matt sits down.

. . . me and God, we got things squared away. I know Jesus died on the cross for us. And I know he's gonna be there to take care of me when I appear before God on Judgement Day.

HELEN

Matt, redemption isn't some kind of free admission ticket that you get because Jesus paid the price. You gotta participate in your own redemption. You got some work to do. I think maybe you should look at the Gospel of John, chapter eight, where Jesus said, 'You shall know the truth and the truth shall make you free.'

MATT

I'll check it out. I like that, the truth shall make you free. I like that. So I pass that lie detector test, I'm home free.

HELEN

Matt, if you do die, as your friend, I wanna help you die with dignity and I don't see how you can do that unless you start to own up to the part you played in Walter and Hope's death.

Matt looks at Helen, whose reflection can be seen in the glass.

EXT. STATE HOUSE. DAY

Hilton walks towards Bishop Norwich and Helen.

HELEN

Hilton Barber, Bishop Norwich.

The two men shake hands.

NORWICH

Hello.

Bishop Norwich, Hilton and Helen walk up the steps towards the state house.

HILTON

Pleasure, Bishop. Uh, now here's the situation. From what I know of Governor Benedict, he is a reluctant supporter of capital punishment. He has the power to stop this execution and save a man's life. It's the last vestige of the divine right of kings. The trick on this is that we have to appeal to him on a personal level, without any fanfare. That's why I've requested a private meeting.

INT. STATE HOUSE. PRESS ROOM. DAY

Hilton and Bishop Norwich sit at a table looking up at Governor Benedict, who faces the room of press and reporters.

GOVERNOR

You must understand that in representing the state . . .

We see the Governor's face on a monitor.

. . . I must carry out the laws and must submerge my own personal views to carry out the express will of the people. I'll look carefully at this case.

Benedict stands at the podium speaking into a group of microphones.

But unless there's some clear, striking evidence for innocence, I will not interfere with the process.

INT. STATE HOUSE. HALLWAY. DAY

Helen looks up as Hilton enters.

HILTON

We still got the court, Sister. We might hit pay dirt on one of the legal issues.

The two walk on, Bishop Norwich following behind them.

INT. PREJEAN'S MOTHER'S HOUSE. BEDROOM. NIGHT

Helen lies on the bed.

HELEN'S MOTHER
(*off*)

Helen? Helen, come to dinner.

Helen rolls over and starts to get out of bed.

You're looking for a love that's so . . .

PREJEAN'S MOTHER'S HOUSE. INT. HALLWAY. NIGHT

Helen walks down the hallway.

HELEN'S MOTHER
(*voice-over*)

. . . big it takes in all evil.

IMAGINED

Matt sits at the dining room table with Helen's brother, her sister, and mother. Sitting across from him are Hope and Walter.

HELEN'S MOTHER
(*voice-over*)

Annunciations . . . are common.

Walter and Hope turn around.

Incarnations are rare. You're not a saint, Helen.

The camera pans to reveal a flashback of nine-year-old Helen standing with a stick in her hand. She is crying.

FLASHBACK – PREJEAN'S MOTHER'S HOUSE. BEDROOM. NIGHT

Helen's mother sits on the bed looking at nine-year-old Helen lying in bed crying.

HELEN'S MOTHER

Helen. Helen.

Nine-year-old Helen breathes heavily.

INT. PREJEAN'S MOTHER'S HOUSE. BEDROOM. NIGHT

Helen's mother looks down at Helen.

HELEN'S MOTHER

Helen.

Helen lies in bed looking up at her mother.

Helen.

HELEN

Oh, Momma. Oh.

Helen's mother rubs Helen's arm.

HELEN'S MOTHER

Are you okay?

HELEN

(*sighs*)

Oh, yes. I was just dreaming.

HELEN'S MOTHER

What time do you have to be there?

HELEN

Nine sharp.

HELEN'S MOTHER

Did you set a clock?

Helen nods.

HELEN

Yeah. Oh, it's so bizarre. A man's gonna be killed in front of me tomorrow.

HELEN'S MOTHER

Has he admitted anything?

HELEN

Oh, no. He's so full of hate, he doesn't trust anybody. He keeps pushing me away.

HELEN'S MOTHER

You're in deep water, kid. Do you remember when you gave me a black eye?

HELEN

I had a fever.

HELEN'S MOTHER

You were delirious, hysterical, screaming. You were tryin' to get up and run into the street. You socked me in the eye and you said you hated me. You screamed, but I held you, I held you tight. 'Cause a mother's arms are strong when her child's in danger.

Helen lies in bed. Her mother looks down at her and puts out her hand. Helen takes it.

EXT. PREJEAN'S MOTHER'S HOUSE. FRONT PORCH

Helen sits on the front porch looking off into the distance.

MATT
(*voice-over*)

I didn't sleep at all last night.

INT. DEATH HOUSE. DAWN

Through the window, we see Matt.

MATT

I didn't take that nerve medicine they wanted to give me. I'm lookin' death in the eyes. I mean, I'm gettin' ready to go.

Helen looks through the window at Matt.

HELEN

Listen, Matt, I want you to know that I respect your need for privacy. If you wanna be alone, or you want to be just with your family today, I understand. I won't be offended.

MATT

You should be there, ma'am, if it won't put you out too much. I'm gonna want somebody to talk to and be there up to the end.

HELEN

I'll be there.

MATT

If only I knew I would die right away with the first shot. I don't know. I mean, will I feel it? The lungs go first. Like a . . . fast choke. That's gotta hurt. They say that, uh . . . the body doesn't move. Doesn't shake.

Helen and Matt look at each other. Matt sniffs.

My poor mama.

INT. ROOM ADJACENT TO BELIVEAU'S OFFICE. DAY

A man is recording the needle marks on the lie detector machine.

HELEN

(*off*)

Any word from the Fifth Circuit?

HILTON

(*over telephone*)

None yet. That's a good sign. They've had it a good while now, maybe that means they see something substantive in the petition.

INT. BELIVEAU'S OFFICE. DAY

Beliveau sits in a chair looking up at Helen, who talks on the phone. Matt can be seen through the window in the adjacent room.

HILTON

(*over telephone*)

Oh, I gotta go. Uh, I'll call you later.

HELEN

(*into telephone*)

Thanks, Hilton.

HILTON

Bye.

HELEN

Bye.

Helen hangs up the phone.

BELIVEAU

Tell me something, Sister.

Helen looks at Beliveau.

What is a nun doing in a place like this? Shouldn't you be teachin' children? Do you know what this man has done? How he killed them kids?

HELEN

What he was involved with was evil. I don't condone it. I just don't see the sense in killin' people to say killin' people's wrong.

BELIVEAU

You know how the Bible says an eye for an eye.

HELEN

You know what else the Bible asks for? Death as a punishment for adultery, prostitution, homosexuality, trespass upon sacred ground, profaning the Sabbath, and contempt of parents.

BELIVEAU

I ain't gonna get in no Bible quoting with no nun, 'cause I'm gonna lose.

Helen smiles.

EXT. DEATH HOUSE. DAY

The strap down team practices leading a prisoner.

We hear Matt and his brothers laughing.

INT. DEATH HOUSE. VISITING ROOM. DAY

Helen looks out of the window.

We hear Matt and his brothers laughing.

We see Matt sitting in a chair facing his family. Matt's stepbrothers, Craig and Sonny, sit on the sofa. Lucille and Troy sit in chairs. Helen sits in a chair, a guard is standing behind her. Helen's reflection can be seen in the window.

CRAIG

She was only on the phone a few minutes and there she was falling for the old Matt charm. I had to take back that phone, trying to steal my gal. You dog.

MATT

She sounds like a great little gal.

CRAIG

Yeah. She is.

SONNY

She ain't so little though.

Craig playfully hits Sonny.

CRAIG

Shut up.

MATT

(*chuckles*)

Now, you take care of her, Craig. Don't do nothin' stupid.

CRAIG

She looks a little bit like, um, come on, what was that girlfriend you had in high school?

MATT

I had lots of girls in high school.

CRAIG

No, the one with the funny name.

MATT

Funny name?

CRAIG

Maddie, Maldy . . . Maldy? Maldy.

MATT

Madrigal.

CRAIG

Madrigal. Madrigal. Madrigal Parmelee. Oh, she was hot.

MATT
(*chuckles*)

She was a nasty little thing.

Troy looks at Lucille, who looks at Matt.

LUCILLE

Matthew.

MATT

Sorry, Ma. I mean, she was a fine upstanding young woman.

Craig claps his hands.

Craig and Sonny laugh.

Matt chuckles.

How 'bout you, Troy?

Lucille looks at Troy, who looks at Matt.

Got yourself a little girlfriend?

TROY

No.

MATT

Why not?

TROY

I ain't got time for girls. Too much fishing and camping to do.

LUCILLE

Troy just got a new tent.

MATT

What kinda tent you got?

TROY

Army tent. I don't like them sissy ones with all them colors.

SONNY

Tell Matt about that other night in the back yard.

CRAIG

The camping in the back yard.

TROY
(*overlapping*)
What are you talking about?

LUCILLE
Oh, I made him come in. I was worried. I just went out there and I made him come inside.

CRAIG
Mama, that ain't what happened.

SONNY
Go on. Then what? Go on. Tell him.

CRAIG
Come on.

TROY
(*sighs*)
Me and my buddy Paul put up this tent, cooked our own dinner.

CRAIG
Come on.

SONNY
Go on.

TROY
We roasted potatoes in tin foil on the fire and cooked us some weenies.

SONNY
Then what? Heh. Go on.

TROY
About midnight . . .

CRAIG
No, about nine o'clock, I think.

SONNY
Yeah.

TROY
. . . we heard some kind of animal.

CRAIG

What kinda animal was that?

TROY

It was big.

CRAIG

Was it a bunny?

SONNY

Was it a possum?

TROY

Shut up.

CRAIG

Was it a, a squirrel?

SONNY

Was it a mouse?

Helen tries to keep from laughing.

Helen laughs.

TROY

Shut up. It was big and nasty.

MATT

Hey, look me in the eye, little man. Did you go inside 'cause Mama told you to, or 'cause you were scared?

CRAIG

Now, tell the truth.

Sonny and Craig look at Troy.

Matt points at Troy.

MATT

Look me in the eye.

Troy smiles.

The boys laugh.

We got him.

Craig claps his hands together.

Lucille looks at Troy and smiles.

Lucille looks at Matt.

LUCILLE

Some people are askin' about your funeral and I get real angry and I say, 'He's not dead yet.'

Sonny and Craig look down, depressed.

Matt sits back and looks up.

Troy looks at Matt.

Matt looks away.

Helen looks around uncomfortably. She looks up at the clock.

Helen sighs.

The clock reads 2:20.

EXT. DEATH HOUSE. DAY

An empty field. Sunset.

INT. DEATH HOUSE. VISITING ROOM. DAY

Helen looks out of a window. Lucille sits in a chair wiping her tears with a tissue. Troy enters. Matt sits in a chair. Sonny sits on the sofa. Helen stands beside her looking out the window. Troy paces to and fro, squeaking his tennis shoes along the floor as he walks. The door opens and Hartman enters.

HARTMAN

I'm sorry, folks. We're gonna . . .

Matt looks around.

. . . have to wrap this up.

MATT

It's a little early, isn't it? Rules say they can stay till six forty-five.

Hartman looks at the clock.

The clock on the wall reads 6:33.

It's time for you folks to be leaving now.

Everyone looks at Hartman, who stands at the door. He exits.

Matt sits back in his chair. He sighs.

Troy stands in the middle of the room surrounded by the others.

Trapp enters carrying two white bags. He walks to Matt and sets the white bags by Matt's chair.

TRAPP

Here you go, Poncelet.

MATT

Thanks, man. Yeah, I got all my stuff in these two pillowcases. I'd like it better if y'all took it home with ya.

Troy stands in the middle of the room looking at Matt. The others surround him.

Don't want the prison sendin' it. Craig, you can divide up all the stuff, except my boots from Marion. I want to walk to my execution in these here boots.

The camera tilts down to Matt's boots.

BELIVEAU

(*off*)

Up on your feet.

Matt is helped up by two guards. He faces Helen and his family members as other guards move in around him.

(*on screen*)

You all say your goodbyes now.

Matt is held under each arm by two guards. Two more guards stand behind him.

Matt's family and Helen walk towards him.

CRAIG

See you later, Matt.

TROY

Bye.

MATT

No goodbyes, little man.

Lucille walks forward, standing beside Troy. Beliveau and another guard stop her from going any further.

BELIVEAU

No, ma'am.

HELEN

Can't she hug him?

Matt, held by two guards, looks around.

BELIVEAU

I'm sorry, Sister. Security reasons.

Lucille and Troy look up at Matt.

MATT

Don't cry, Mama. I don't wanna see no cryin'. I'm not sayin' goodbye now. I'll call you tonight.

The guards lead Matt away.

CRAIG

See ya, Matt. Stay strong.

MATT

Don't cry, Mama. I'll call you later.

LUCILLE

We love you, Mattie.

Helen puts her arms around Lucille and they walk out.

INT. DEATH HOUSE. HALLWAY. DUSK

Helen and Lucille walk down the hallway. Helen has her arm around Lucille.

LUCILLE

(*crying*)

If I'd put my arms around my boy, I'd never have let go.

EXT. DEATH HOUSE. FRONT DOOR. DUSK

Lucille walks out of the door. Helen stands inside as the door closes. Lucille, Craig and Sonny walk toward their truck. Troy waves at Helen. She waves back, as Lucille falls onto the hood of the truck, sobbing.

Matt is led away by two guards. He peeks back as he walks.

MATT

Is my mama all right?

Helen turns away from the door and looks at Matt.

HELEN

She's fine, Matt.

INT. DEATH HOUSE. SUNSET

A guard sits watching TV. Helen talks on a pay phone.

HELEN

(*into telephone*)

All right. Goodbye.

Helen hangs up and walks toward Matt's cell. She sits down.

A TV Sports Announcer does play-by-play of a baseball game.

TV SPORTS ANNOUNCER

(*voice-over*)

Well, you know, John . . .

The sound of the TV continues under the following scene.

MATT

I never had shrimp before.

Matt is eating his last meal.

They're pretty good. So what did it say? What's the word on the lie detector test?

HELEN

Culp said your answers showed stress, just as he predicted, and the results were inconclusive.

MATT

Man. Was the dude sure? Absolutely, positively sure? I felt all right answering them questions. I didn't feel no stress. I can't believe I failed that test.

HELEN

Matt, you'd have to be a robot or insane not to feel stress now.

MATT

I can't believe that test didn't come out right.

Helen leans forward.

HELEN

Let's talk about what happened. Let's talk about that night.

MATT

I don't wanna talk about that.

Helen looks at Matt. She then sits back and looks up at the clock. The clock on the wall reads 8:29. The camera unfocuses, creating a blur.

FLASHBACK – EXT. LOUISIANA WOODS. NIGHT

The camera dollies past trees toward a parked car.

Inside, Hope and Walter are necking. The camera pans to reveal Matt looking in the window at them.

Vitello looks down into the car.

Matt looks into the car at Hope and Walter kissing. Walter looks at Matt.

MATT

Get outta the car.

VITELLO
(*off*)

Hey . . .

Vitello looks down into the car at Hope.

. . . you're a pretty bunny.

MATT

Trespassing.

Matt looks in the car at Walter.

WALTER

What?

MATT

You're trespassing. This is private property.

Vitello looks in the window at Hope.

HOPE

Let's go.

VITELLO

You're under arrest. Step out of the car.

WALTER

We'll just . . .

Matt looks down at Walter.

. . . leave. We didn't know it was private property.

Matt opens the car door. Walter looks at Hope.

MATT
(*shouting*)

Get outta the car!

Hope and Walter look stunned with fright.

CUT TO:

Vitello leads a handcuffed Hope, followed by a handcuffed Walter led by Matt.

WALTER

Where are we going?

VITELLO

Oh, there's a little bar back here somewhere. Heh.

WALTER

Our boss is in the bar.

VITELLO

Yeah, can't let you go though, you've been bad.

WALTER

Our boss is gonna be pissed.

VITELLO

Yeah, but maybe he'll let you go.

The four walk in the woods.

Well. Here we are. This is the bar. Can we get you a drink? Kneel down.

Vitello pushes Hope to her knees.

INT. DEATH HOUSE. NIGHT

From a blur, the camera refocuses on the clock on the wall, which reads 10:31.

We see Matt through the cell bars.

MATT

I'm pissed off! I'm pissed off at them kids for bein' parked out in the woods that night. Pissed off at their parents comin' to see me die. Pissed off at myself for lettin' Vitello get over on them kids. But I got my last words coming. And I got a thing or two to say to the Percys and the Delacroixs.

HELEN

You want your last words to be words of hatred?

MATT

(*shouting*)

Hey! Clyde Percy said he wants to inject me hisself!

HELEN

Well, think of how angry he must be. He's never gonna see his daughter again. He's never gonna hold her. He's never gonna love her, laugh with her. You have robbed these parents of so much, Matt. They have nothing in their lives but sorrow, no joy. That is what you have given them.

Matt looks around.

What possessed you to be in the woods that night?

MATT

I told ya, I was stoned outta my head!

HELEN

Now don't blame the drugs. You were harassing couples for weeks before this happened. Months! What was it?

MATT

What do you mean?

HELEN

Did you look up to Vitello? Did you think he was cool?

Matt leans against the wall.

Did you wanna impress him?

MATT

I don't know.

HELEN

You could have just walked away.

MATT

Hey, he went psycho on me.

HELEN

Don't blame him. You blame him. You blame the government. You blame drugs. You blame blacks. You blame the Percys. You blame the kids for being there. What about Matthew Poncelet? Where's he in this story? What, is he just an innocent? A victim?

MATT

I ain't no victim.

Matt walks back and forth. He hears a door open.

Helen looks towards the sound.

Hartman walks in, followed by Beliveau and other guards.

HARTMAN

Poncelet.

Matt looks down.

Hartman steps forward, followed by Beliveau and two other guards.

Helen looks at Hartman.

Hartman looks at Matt.

Federal Appeals Court turned you down. I'm sorry.

Hartman walks away.

Through the cell bars, Matt looks at Hartman walking away.

Through the cell bars, Helen looks towards Hartman and then towards Matt.

BELIVEAU
(*off*)

Sister, please step into the corridor.

HELEN

I'll be right outside.

INT. DEATH HOUSE. HALLWAY. NIGHT

Helen and Beliveau walk to the desk. Helen turns and looks through the window at Matt, who talks on the phone.

HILTON
(*over telephone*)

Matt?

MATT
(*into telephone*)

Yeah.

HILTON

The Fifth Circuit Court judge . . .

Helen watches.

I'm sorry, son. I feel like I failed.

MATT

No, you didn't fail. You didn't. I appreciate everything you and the others have done for me.

Helen looks at Beliveau, who is filling out some forms.

MATT

I shoulda got you sooner . . .

HELEN

What is she typing?

BELIVEAU

Uh, forms for the witnesses to sign.

Helen walks away.

MATT

Well, you didn't fail. The justice system in this country failed. It stinks. It stinks bad.

HILTON

Well, I'm gonna head out there right now.

INT. DEATH HOUSE FOYER/VISITING ROOM. NIGHT

Two guards place a tablecloth on a table. Helen enters and walks through the visiting room into the ladies' room.

INT. LADIES' ROOM. NIGHT

Helen enters.

HELEN

Oh, God, help me.

Helen paces back and forth. We see Helen's reflection in the mirror as she leans her head against the wall in distress.

This is such a terrifying place, Lord. So cold. So calculated, this murder. Just don't let him fall apart, God. Oh, help him stay strong. Help me, Jesus, stay strong. Help us, Lord.

A nurse enters.

Help us stay strong. Help me.

Helen breathes heavily. She realizes she is being watched. She steps up to the sink as the nurse walks away.

INT. DEATH HOUSE. MATT'S CELL. DAY

Matt sits on a cot. Helen approaches.

MATT

They shaved the calf of my leg.

Helen looks down.

HELEN

Why?

MATT

I guess they was worried they won't find a vein in my arm.

HELEN

What's that number?

There is a tattoo on Matt's leg. It reads: 4-8-58.

MATT

I put it on there when I was at Marion. In case somebody killed me, they could identify my body.

Helen looks at the tattoos on Matt's arm.

HELEN

Did it hurt when you did all those?

Matt looks down.

MATT

You seeing these tattoos, you gonna think I'm a bad person.

HELEN

Nah, you just have a little more color on your body than I thought.

Matt looks down.

MATT

Tried to give me two shots.

Matt sits up on his cot.

A sedative and an antihistamine.

HELEN

Antihistamine?

MATT

Yeah. Guess, uh, if I had an allergic reaction to the first shot that knocks you out, it gets messy. Come on, I wanna give you . . .

Matt gets up and walks over to Helen.

. . . my Bible. I dated it myself.

Matt passes the Bible through the bars to her. Helen looks touched.

HELEN

Hey, thanks, Matt.

GUARD

(*off*)

Stand back from the cell, Sister.

MATT

Time to call home. Will you stay?

HELEN

I'll stay, I'll just give you some privacy.

Helen exits. A guard (*hands only*) *enters and sets the phone on the chair.*

Helen sits listening to Matt's conversation.

MATT

Hey, man.

CRAIG

(*over telephone*)

What you doin'?

MATT

(*into telephone*)

Heh. You know what I'm doin'. What are you doing?

Craig's voice is indistinct. Matt is sniffing.

Yeah.

Helen glances toward the visitors' room.

It . . . The time's ticking away.

Through the window, a man eats a sandwich. Other men talk.

TROY

(*over telephone*)

Hey . . .

MATT

Hey. (*Sniffs.*) What you doin' grabbin' the phone? (*Chuckles.*)

TROY

Yep.

MATT

Gonna sleep in your tent tonight?

Helen looks away, tears filling her eyes.

TROY

Yeah, I am.

MATT

Oh.

LUCILLE

(*over telephone*)

Hello.

MATT

Hey, Mom, I'm waitin' to talk to ya. Don't cry, Mom.

Helen looks at Matt, her eyes filled with tears.

(*sniffling*)

Don't cry. Don't cry.

Lucille sobs over the telephone.

The clock on the wall reads 11:29.

Don't.

Craig's voice is heard indistinctly over the telephone.

Helen looks at the Bible Matt gave her.

They . . . They thought I would. I was . . .

Helen opens the book revealing 'Wife's family tree'. She turns the page.

I was small.

The Bible page is titled: Record of Deaths. Matt has written his name on the page.

MATTHEW PONCELET
4/13/94
ANGOLA

It had nothing to do with that guy.

Lucille's voice is heard indistinctly over the telephone.

Yeah, I could hear him. Lemme, let me talk to him. Hey, Troy. You take care of Momma, okay? All right, little man.

TROY

All right.

MATT

You take care of Momma.

(*off*)

Mom? Mom?

Lucille weeps over the telephone.

(*sniffing*)

I love you, Mom. I love you, Mom.

INT. DEATH HOUSE. OUTSIDE MATT'S CELL. NIGHT

The clock on the wall reads 11:37.

MATT

I just let it flow.

Matt hangs his head. Helen looks at him through the cell bars.

Told my mama I loved her. I talked to each of the boys. I hate saying goodbye. I just told 'em if I get a chance, I'd call right before I go.

Helen holds onto the bars, looking at Matt.

HELEN

What, Matt? What is it?

Matt hangs his head, then looks up at Helen as he speaks.

MATT

My mama kept saying it was that Vitello. I should always regret that I got involved with him. I didn't want her thinkin' that. It was somethin' that you said. I coulda walked away. I didn't. I was a victim. I was a fuckin' chicken. He was older and tough as hell. I was just . . . boozin' up, trying to be as tough as him. I couldn't. I didn't have the guts to stand up to him. I told my mama I was yellow. She kept saying, 'It wasn't you, Matt. It wasn't you, Matt. It wasn't you.'

HELEN

Your mama loves you, Matt.

MATT

The boy, Walter . . .

HELEN

(*softly*)

Yeah? What?

MATT

I killed him.

HELEN

And Hope?

MATT

No, ma'am.

HELEN

Did you rape her?

Matt looks at Helen and then looks down, his eyes starting to fill with tears.

MATT
(*sniffing*)

Yes, ma'am.

HELEN
(*exhaling*)

Do you take responsibility for both of their deaths?

MATT

Yes, ma'am. When the lights dimmed on the tier last night I kneeled down by my bunk and I prayed for them kids. I never done that before.

Helen gasps.

Matt sniffles.

HELEN

Oh, Matt . . .

Helen closes her eyes as she speaks.

There are spaces of sorrow only God can touch. You did a terrible thing, Matt, a terrible thing. But you have a dignity now. Nobody can take that from you. You are a son of God, Matthew Poncelet.

MATT

Yeah.

Matt hangs his head and cries. He looks up at Helen, fighting back tears.

Nobody ever called me no son of God before. Called me a son of you-know-whats lot of times, never no son of God.

Helen chuckles.

I just hope my death can give them parents some relief. I really do.

HELEN

Well, maybe it's the best thing you can give to the Percys and the Delacroixs is a wish for their peace.

MATT

(*sniffing*)

You know I never had no . . . no real love myself. Never loved a woman or anybody else myself much good. It figures I'd have to die to find love.

Helen breathes heavily.

Thank you for loving me.

Helen looks at Matt. Tears stream down her cheek.

We hear a guard laugh.

Matt looks at the clock. It reads 11:41.

Look at the time. It's been flying. I'm really cold.

Helen looks at a guard.

HELEN

Can he have a jacket or something? He's cold.

MATT

Hey, what happened to that song you were gonna play for me?

HELEN

The hymn?

MATT

Uh-huh.

HELEN

(*sighs*)

They have a rule you can't have music in the prison.

MATT

Yeah.

HELEN

Yeah, so they won't let me play it.

MATT

Well, you know the words. You can sing it.

HELEN

I can't sing.

MATT

That's okay. Come on.

HELEN

(*breathy singing*)

'If you pass through raging waters of the sea, you shall not drown. If you walk amid the burning flames, you shall not be harmed. If you stand beside the power of Hell and death is by your side, know that I will be there through it all. Be not . . .

Matt rests his head on the cell bars.

. . . afraid. I go before you always. Come follow me and I will give you rest.'

MATT

Thank you.

Helen shuts her eyes.

GUARD

(*off*)

I need you to step into the corridor, Sister.

Matt looks at Helen.

Helen turns to get up.

Matt starts to cry, breathing deeply.

INT. DEATH HOUSE. CORRIDOR. NIGHT

Helen backs away from the door. As she steps forward she notices Mr Delacroix.

Through the window to an adjoining corridor, Mr Delacroix looks at Helen. Mary Beth Percy and others are also present. All walk toward the door. Farley walks in.

Helen glances toward a window. A light turns on, revealing Matt in his cell, surrounded by guards. Matt tries to look out through the window at Helen.

INT. DEATH HOUSE. MATT'S CELL. NIGHT

A guard opens the door to reveal Beliveau picking up Matt's boots. Beliveau and a guard walk away, revealing Matt being held under the arms by two guards.

MATT

Give me back my boots! I want my boots! A grown man going to his death in a diaper and slippers.

The two guards lead Matt forward toward the execution room.

I'll be done with all of this! No more bars, no more cells, no more life in a cage!

Helen looks at Matt. Beliveau and Hartman are behind her.

HELEN

Matt.

MATT

Sister Helen . . .

Matt collapses, supported by two guards.

. . . I'm gonna die.

HELEN

You know the truth. The truth has made you free.

Matt hangs his head and looks down at Helen.

MATT

God knows the truth about me. I'm going to a better place. I'm not worried about nothin'.

HELEN

(*low*)

No.

MATT

You all right?

Helen looks up at Matt and nods.

HELEN

Yes. I'm okay. Christ is here.

MATT

I'm not worried about anything.

HELEN

Okay. Look, I want the last thing you see in this world to be a face of love.

Matt looks down at Helen, and starts to cry.

So you look at me when they do this thing. You look at me. I'll be the face of love for you.

MATT

Yes, ma'am.

HARTMAN

(*off*)

Time to go, Poncelet.

Matt is lifted to his feet by two guards.

Matt looks at Helen.

MATT

Can Sister Helen touch me?

Helen looks at Matt. Beliveau and Hartman stand behind her.

HARTMAN

Yes, she may.

Helen starts to move forward.

Helen enters and puts her hand on Matt's shoulder. Beliveau enters.

BELIVEAU

Dead man walking!

He walks on, followed by Matt, the guards, Helen and Trapp.

INT. DEATH HOUSE CORRIDOR. NIGHT

Matt is led by two guards. Helen follows behind.

Slow motion begins. Matt (slippered feet only) walks slowly, handcuffs around his ankles.

Matt (hands only) walks on, his hands handcuffed. We see a diaper beneath his pants.

Helen (hand only) holds his shoulder.

Helen looks at Matt as they walk.

HELEN

Do not be afraid.

Slow motion ends. Helen reads from the Bible and looks at Matt as they walk.

'For I have ordained thee, I have called thee by thy name. Thou art mine. Should thou pass through the sea, I shall be with thee.'

Matt walks on, followed by Helen and other guards.

'Should thou walk through the fire . . .'

INT. CORRIDOR OUTSIDE EXECUTION ROOM. NIGHT

Matt is led down the corridor, followed by Helen and guards.

HELEN

'. . . thou shall not be scorched. I have . . .'

FARLEY

May God have mercy on your . . .

Farley gives a blessing.

FARLEY and HELEN

(*off-screen*)

. . . soul in the name of the Father, the Son and the Holy Spirit.

Beliveau enters.

BELIVEAU

That's as far . . .

Matt and Helen walk and stop.

. . . as you go, Sister.

Matt looks at Helen.

MATT

Will you check in on my mama from time to time?

Helen nods.

HELEN

Yes, Matt. You have my word on that.

She kisses Matt's shoulder as he walks away. She stares off after him, until a guard gently turns her toward the door. She walks through and sits down beside Hilton. Members of the press are seated behind them.

INT. EXECUTION ROOM/OBSERVATION ROOM. NIGHT

Helen looks at Hilton, the Percys, and Mr Delacroix.

Mary Beth and Clyde sit facing front. Mr Delacroix sits behind them. They all glance at Helen. A reporter is taking notes.

Hilton is sitting next to Helen. Both look at the clock on the wall. It reads 11:54.

INT. EXECUTION ROOM. NIGHT

The camera tilts up from the floor to Matt's legs as two guards (hands only) buckle a belt, strapping his legs down.

Two guards buckle a belt.

A guard (hands only) removes the handcuff harness from Matt. Camera tilts up as two guards (hands only) buckle a harness on Matt (chest only), and continues to tilt up to Matt's face.

A guard (hands only) straps down Matt's arm, and lowers the arm of the gurney. Camera pans to the nurse who treated Helen earlier.

Matt looks down. The camera rotates and pans to reveal the nurse (gloved hands only) tying a tourniquet around Matt's arm. She swabs a spot on his arm with alcohol, pushes a needle into it, and tapes the needle down. She then attaches the intravenous tube to the needle. The camera pans and rotates up to Matt's face. The clock on the wall reads 11:57.

INT. EXECUTION ROOM/OBSERVATION ROOM. NIGHT

Beliveau pulls back the curtain of the observation window to reveal Matt strapped to the lethal injection gurney. Hartman and guards stand around him.

Helen looks at Matt.

HARTMAN
(*off*)
Do you have any last words, Poncelet?

Matt looks around at Mr Delacroix.

MATT
Yes, sir, I do. Mr Delacroix . . .

Mr Delacroix looks at Matt.

. . . I don't want to leave this world with any hate in my heart.

Matt looks at Mr Delacroix.

(*shaking*)

I ask your forgiveness for what I done. It was a terrible thing I done taking your son away from you.

Mr Delacroix listens. Clyde Percy looks at Mary Beth.

CLYDE

How 'bout us?

MATT

Mr and Mrs Percy, I hope my death gives you some relief.

Helen has tears in her eyes.

Matt looks around. He is still shaking.

I just want to say, I think killing is wrong, no matter who does it. Whether it's me or y'all or your government.

Hartman enters and crosses in front of Matt. The guards tip the lethal injection gurney back, laying it flat.

Helen has tears in her eyes.

The guards turn the gurney.

Matt lies on his back as the gurney turns and stops. He looks at Helen.

Helen looks at Matt.

Matt lies on his back looking toward Helen.

I love you.

Through the observation window, Hilton and Helen look at Matt, whose reflection can be seen in the glass. Helen mouths 'I love you' to Matt, and reaches out her hand.

Matt lies on his back looking at Helen.

Beliveau looks at Hartman, who looks up at the clock on the wall. It reads 12:00. The camera tilts down to reveal Hartman, who looks at Beliveau.

Beliveau and Trapp stand at the lethal injection machine. Matt lies on the gurney. Beliveau looks at Trapp.

Trapp looks back at Beliveau as they both (hands only) flip the switch on the machine. The two walk out, followed by Hartman.

FLASHBACK – EXT. LOUISIANA WOODS. NIGHT

The camera dollies from behind a tree to reveal Vitello straddling Hope, tearing off her clothes. Matt is in the background with his foot on Walter, who lies on the ground.

The camera dollies past trees as Vitello gets up and takes the gun from Matt. Matt walks and stands over Hope, gyrating his hips and undoing his pants.

INT. EXECUTION ROOM/OBSERVATION ROOM. NIGHT

Through the observation window, Helen reaches out to Matt, whose reflection can be seen in the glass. Hilton sits, his head bowed.

Matt lies on the gurney looking at Helen.

We see the controls on the lethal injection machine.

One of the controls reads: 'armed'. Camera tilts down to a 'start' button that lights up.

A row of syringes begin to inject a lethal fluid.

Through the observation window, Helen looks at Matt, whose reflection can be seen in the glass.

The fluid moves through the tube, camera panning with it.

Matt lies on the gurney looking at Helen.

Through the observation window, Helen looks at Matt, whose reflection can be seen in the glass.

Two syringes, the left empty, the right injecting a lethal fluid.

The camera pans up the tube to Matt's arm and tilts up to his face.

We see Helen's face (eyes and nose only).

FLASHBACK – LOUISIANA WOODS. NIGHT

Walter lies face down on the ground in pain.

Vitello looks down maniacally at Walter.

Matt rapes Hope.

Vitello pulls Matt off Hope, and hands him the gun.

Matt takes the gun from Vitello, who takes down his pants to rape Hope, camera dollying behind a tree.

Vitello takes out a knife and stabs Hope repeatedly.

WALTER
(*shouts*)

No!

Matt looks around nervously, and aims the gun down at Walter.

No! Ahhh!!! Ahhhh!

Matt (foot only) steps on Walter's back and shoots him in the back of the head.

INT. EXECUTION ROOM/OBSERVATION ROOM. NIGHT

We see two syringes; the left empty, the right injects the remainder of its lethal fluid.

Matt lies on the gurney looking at Helen. His eyes start to close woozily.

Through the observation window, Helen looks and mouths 'I love you' to Matt, whose reflection can be seen in the glass.

Through the observation window, Mary Beth and Clyde look at Matt. Mr Delacroix sits behind them.

Matt (hand only) goes limp. Matt's eyes close.

Through the observation window, Helen looks at Matt, whose reflection can be seen in the glass. She slowly lowers her arm.

FLASHBACK – EXT. LOUISIANA WOODS. NIGHT.

Matt hands the gun to Vitello, who points it down at Hope and shoots.

INT. EXECUTION ROOM/OBSERVATION ROOM. NIGHT

We see a row of syringes. One releases a lethal fluid.

Through the observation window, Hilton and Helen look at Matt, whose reflection can be seen in the glass.

We see the control board of the machine.

We see a row of syringes.

We see a row of hydraulic cylinders.

Through the observation window, Helen closes her eyes and prays to herself. Matt's reflection can be seen in the glass.

The camera pans up the tube.

We see two syringes. The right injects lethal fluid.

The camera tilts up from the needle in Matt's arm to his lifeless face.

FLASHBACK – EXT. LOUISIANA WOODS. NIGHT

Vitello and Matt run away, disappearing into the woods.

INT. EXECUTION ROOM/OBSERVATION ROOM. NIGHT

Through the observation window, Matt's lifeless body lies on the gurney. Walter and Hope's reflections can be seen in the glass.

A syringe empties the final amount of lethal fluid.

We see the controls on the lethal injection machine.

We see the 'finish' button.

Through the observation window, Helen prays to herself, her eyes closed. Matt's reflection can be seen in the glass.

We see Helen's face (eyes and nose only).

We see Matt's lifeless face. His eyes fall open.

FLASHBACK – EXT. LOUISIANA WOODS. DAY

The camera pans over the tree-lined bog and tilts down for an aerial view, to reveal Hope and Walter's lifeless bodies lying naked on the ground below.

INT. EXECUTION ROOM. NIGHT. AERIAL VIEW

Matt's lifeless body lies on the gurney, camera rotating and pulling back.

BISHOP NORWICH
(*voice-over*)
May the love of God and the peace of our dear Lord Jesus Christ bless us and console us . . .

DISSOLVE TO:

EXT. CEMETERY. DAY

The camera tilts up from the ground, past a casket, to Matt's brothers, and continues on to reveal Lucille, Helen and Bishop Norwich.

BISHOP NORWICH

. . . and gently wipe every tear from our eyes. Amen. May Almighty God bless you, the Father, the Son, and the Holy Spirit. Amen.

CRAIG/SONNY

Amen.

BISHOP NORWICH

Go now in the peace and love of Christ.

HELEN and OTHERS

Thanks be to God.

Helen places a flower on the casket. She looks at Lucille and hugs her. The other mourners and Bishop Norwich mill about. Helen kisses Troy on the head and walks to Sonny.

HELEN

I know you're gonna be strong for your mama.

Helen hugs Sonny.

Mr Delacroix stands by his car.

Helen hugs Sonny, looking at Mr Delacroix. She pulls away and walks toward him. Lucille and Troy look down at the casket. Craig stands at the head of the casket, pouring a bottle of beer on it as Sonny looks on.

EXT. CEMETERY. DAY

Helen walks back to Mr Delacroix.

HELEN

Mr Delacroix.

MR DELACROIX

Sister.

HELEN

It's good to see you.

MR DELACROIX

I don't know why I'm here. I got a lot of hate. I don't have your faith.

HELEN

It's not faith. I wish it was that easy. It's work. Maybe we could help each other find a way outta the hate.

MR DELACROIX

I don't know. I don't think so. I should go.

Mr Delacroix starts to turn away.

Helen looks at Mr Delacroix as he walks to his car.

EXT. STREET OUTSIDE THE HOPE HOUSE. DAY

Helen gets out of her car. She speaks to women and children, who are off screen.

HELEN

Evenin'.

She walks up the steps past the women and children who sit on them. Idella exits from the house.

HELEN

Hi, Idella.

IDELLA
(*shouting*)

Herbie!

Helen goes into the house.

INT. HOPE HOUSE. STAIRWELL

Helen enters from around a corner. Looking around, she walks up the stairs, camera tilting up and panning off her to a wall of children's drawings. they read:

CHEER UP
SISTER

WE LOVE
YOU SISTER

DON BE
BLUE
HELEN

SMILE

Helen looks at the drawings and smiles, touched.

EXT. OUR LADY OF MERCY CHURCH. DAY

Helen walks toward the quaint country church and disappears inside.

Helen kneels in a pew, praying, with Mr Delacroix at her side. Camera dollies back from the window, past the trees, to reveal the front of the church as end titles fade in and out.

'Dead Man Walking' by Bruce Springsteen plays on soundtrack.